Let My Children Cook!

A Passover cookbook for kids

by Tamar Ansh

Judaica
PRESS

Let My Children Cook!

A Passover cookbook for kids

© 2014 Tamar Ansh

ISBN: 978-1-60763-142-2

Editor: Chumi Leshinsky
Proofreader: Tova Finkelman
Cover and internal design and layout: Avigayil Shapiro
Cover and internal illustrations: Evgeniy Ognarov

THE JUDAICA PRESS, INC.
123 Ditmas Avenue / Brooklyn, NY 11218
718-972-6200 / 800-972-6201
info@judaicapress.com
judaicapress.com

Manufactured in China

Contents

Introduction 5
Important Cooking and Safety Tips 6

Passover VIR's (Very Important Recipes). 8

Charoses. 8
Traditional Fluffy Matzah Balls. 9
Crushed-Matzah Matzah Balls 10
Matzah Soup Squares 11
Miniature Charoses Balls. 12

Fun Finger Foods 13

Fun Kids' Plate Idea 13
Turkey Shishkabobs 14
Roasted Shishkabobs 15
Crispy Potato Shishkabobs 16
Dried Fruit Kabobs. 17
Candy-Stick Kabobs 18

Munch-a-Brunch. 19

Matzah Brie 19
Spicy Matzah Brie 20
Scribbled Eggs 21
Matzah Marshmallow Melt 22
Cheesy Matzah Pie. 23
Matzah Pizza 24
Blueberry Pancakes 25
Blueberry or Peach Muffins. 26
Matzah Meal Rolls 27

Soups & Other Such Stuff 29

Pastel-Colored Soup. 29
Chicken Soup. 30
Thick 'n' Creamy Chicken Soup 31
Potato Soup. 32
Stuffed Matzah Balls 33

Fish Your Own Fish 34

Really Easy Gefilte Fish. 34
Moroccan-Style Gefilte Fish 35
Cucumber Holders 36
Nova Finger Treats. 37
Salmon Latkes 38
Instant Tasty Salmon Steaks. 39

Meat and Chicken 40

Meat Burgers. 40
Easy Sauce Chicken 41
Coated Chicken Shake. 42
Crunchy Chicken Crisps. 43
Really Good, Quick Meatballs in Sauce . . 44
Meatloaf 45
Crispy Chicken Cutlets (CCC's) 46
Spicy Chicken Bake. 47
Barbecue-Flavored Chicken Wings. 48
Surprise Matzah Meatballs in Sauce. . . . 49

Veggies, Salads and Potatoes 50

Israeli Salad 50
Cucumber Salad 51
Coleslaw 52
Fruity Beet Salad. 53
French Fries. 54
Veggie Kabobs. 55
Pizza Potatoes 56
Potato Salad 57
Sweet Potato Puffs 58
Baby Carrot Tzimmes 59

Latkes & Kugels 60

Zucchini Kugel 60
Potato Latkes 61
Cheese Latkes 62
Potato Kugel 63
Butternut Squash Kugel 64

Fruits & Fruity Desserts 65

Apple Compote 65
Homemade Applesauce 66
Crunchy Cranberry Relish 67
Blended Fruit Soup 68
Stuffed Baked Apples 69
Fruit Cups 70
Frozen Raisin Clusters 71
Coated Banana Freeze Pops 72
Poached Pears 73
Strawberry Soup 74

Cakes, Cookies, and Mmm ... More! 75

Blondies 75
Rocky Road Brownies 76
Chocolate Chip Brownies 77
Passover Apple Crisp 78
Passover Mock Oatmeal Cookies 79
Chocolate Chip Cookies 80

Desserts, Shakes & Drinks 81

Strawberry Snow 81
Chocolate Mousse 82
Marshmallow Dream Ice Cream 83
Easy Vanilla Ice Cream 84
Chocolate Chip Ice Cream 85
Chocolate-Coffee Ice Cream 86
Ice Cream Sundae 86
Incredible Milkshakes 87
Milk-Less Fruit Shakes 88
Homemade Ice Coffee 89
Fresh Lemonade 90
Fro-Yo Ice Pops 90

Fun Arts & Crafts 91

Passover Aprons 91
Passover Placemats 92
Seder Table Pillows 93
Wine Bottle Labels 94

Introduction

To my young readers,

Welcome to my Passover cookbook, "**Let My Children Cook!**" — which is exactly what I plan on helping you do. I've included all sorts of recipes that I thought you'd enjoy and find easy to try. Some recipes are serving ideas and some require real cooking; there's sure to be something for everyone in this book. And some recipes are just really good and traditional food — such as charoses, chicken soup, and potato kugel. I included those, too, since they're such basic foods for Passover. If you really want to be a real cook, well, you've got to learn these kinds of recipes somehow ... and what better way than this great cookbook! I've also included a few fun arts and crafts ideas you can make yourself.

Above all else — enjoy yourself! This book was written so that you, too, can know the accomplishment, delight and satisfaction in making something GOOD, all by yourself. What better time of year to do this than Passover, when families get together and you can really show off your cooking talents ...

Now, go and make yourself your own apron from page 91 and have a GREAT time cooking!

With best wishes to all of you for a *"kosheren* and *freilichen* Pesach" — a really great and happy Passover!

"לשנה הבאה בירושלים הבנויה." Next year may we all be together in Jerusalem, just as we sing at the end of the Passover Seders — and when that happens, stop by and say hello; I'd love to meet you!

All the best,

Tamar Ansh
Jerusalem, Israel
Teves, 5774

Cooking and Safety Tips

Here are some helpful tips before you begin:

- **Always** ask a parent for permission first to make sure it's okay to be cooking in the kitchen.

- **Always** make sure someone else is home with you when you want to cook or bake. And only turn on the flame yourself if your parents allow. Otherwise, ask an adult.

- It's always best to spend a few minutes reading the *entire* recipe before you start. This way you can make sure you have everything you need; your food preparation will go so much smoother and faster if all the necessary ingredients are lined up right near you.

- When you want to move, check on, or open anything hot, use a potholder. Using towels can be dangerous, as they can slip and get caught in the fire under the pot.

- There are nifty little signs near each recipe to help you out — a meat/pareve/dairy or gluten-free symbol for every recipe. According to Jewish dietary laws, we do not eat or cook dairy and meat items for the same meal, and this way, it'll be easy to remember which recipes fit into each category!

- No matter how much little brothers or sisters beg, they should not be allowed anywhere near the hot fire on a stove or a running mixer. Let them help you put things into a bowl instead. Or roll cookies. Or taste-test your yummy food …

- Put your pot of cooking food on the back burners and turn the pot handles towards the back.

- After handling raw chicken, fish, meat or eggs, it is very, very important that you wash your hands with hot water and soap. Any towels that were used to wipe your hands while touching raw food should go into the washing machine. Any utensils you touched or used should go into the sink to be washed as well.

- Make sure there are no crawling babies nearby when you take something out of the oven or off the stovetop.

- Don't leave anything hot on a table or at the edge of a counter, where a small child can climb up and reach it.

- **Always** make sure your hands are totally dry before touching any plugs or outlets. **Always** wear rubber-soled shoes when you plug anything into the outlet.

- A real cook knows that the cooking is not over until every single thing is cleaned up, wiped off and put back in its place!

- **Always** make sure your hands are clean before you begin cooking anything.

- Follow the guidelines of your rabbi/Torah authority for checking dried fruit, fresh fruit, vegetables and other items for bugs before using them. According to Jewish dietary laws, ideally only someone who is bar or bas mitzvah age and above (and who has been taught how) should check food for bugs.

- Lots of fun recipes in this book call for separating eggs. If you don't already know how to separate an egg, have your mom teach you so you can make these recipes. It's a valuable cooking and baking tip to know.

- Only use a food processor or sharp knives when an adult is with you to supervise what you are doing. **Never** do this alone. **Never** put your hands or fingers into a food processor.

- Passover is a time that we are really extra careful with our foods and the kosher certification on them. (Ask your parents about your family customs.) All foods and canned products mentioned in these recipes are available with Kosher for Passover labels on them. All foods prepared for Passover must have these kosher symbols on them, even items such as spices, salt, sugar and the like, in order to be used on Passover. Even matzahs that are used all year long are not used for Passover; many of them can actually be chametz! For Passover we use only matzahs that have been prepared and packaged especially for Passover. The same goes for all the matzah meals, matzah flour, and every other ingredient used. There are tons of choices available nowadays – you should be able to get it all by going to the kosher section of your supermarket.

- Above all else, have a great, happy, tasty and enjoyable Passover! Now, let's BEGIN!

Passover VIR's
(Very Important Recipes)

Charoses

Charoses is a must on every Seder table. After it is made it turns a sort of brownish color, and we eat it to remind us of the cement that the Jews in Egypt had to use when they were slaves. However, their cement was nowhere near as tasty as our charoses "cement" today!

Let's get to it!

3 red apples, peeled
I green apple, peeled
I cup finely chopped walnuts
I teaspoon cinnamon
¼ cup dark red wine

 Pareve

 Makes enough for about 8 Seder participants

And here's how you do it!

1　Peel the apples and cut each one in half. Take out the seeds.

2　Put the apples and walnuts into the food processor and puree them with the "S" blade.

3　Pour the ground apples and nuts into a bowl. Add the cinnamon and dark red wine. Mix it with a spoon and leave it in a covered container until you set the table for the Seder.

Bring your charoses to the Seder table in a pretty glass dish.

Traditional Fluffy Matzah Balls

A.K.A. "Kneidelach"

Let's get to it!

4 eggs, beaten
1 cup matzah meal
½ cup water
⅓ cup oil
½ teaspoon garlic powder, optional
A pinch of salt and pepper

 Meat (in chicken soup)

 Makes about 15-20 balls

And here's how you do it!

1 Beat the eggs in a mixing bowl with a hand beater for a few minutes. Turn off the mixer; add everything else to the beaten eggs and stir with a fork. The mixture will fall a bit; this is fine.

2 Cover the mixture and refrigerate for an hour or overnight.

To prepare the matzah balls:

1 Use a large, wide pot, as these matzah balls will grow a lot in size.

2 Fill the pot 3/4 full with water; boil the water with half a teaspoon of salt until it is bubbling.

3 Wet your hands with a bit of water and shape small balls out of the batter. Drop them gently (the hot liquid can splash!) into the boiling water.

4 Cook for 30–40 minutes. Remove the matzah balls from the pot with a slotted spoon. Place them on a flat plate and let them cool.

5 Freeze your fluffy matzah balls in plastic bags or a container. When you are ready to use them, drop them into your family's boiling chicken soup while they are still frozen. Half an hour later they will be fluffy, soft and ready to eat!

Another idea is to use a mini ice-cream scooper or a mini cookie-baller to shape the matzah balls, so that every matzah ball will be the same size.

Crushed-Matzah Matzah Balls

Let's get to it!

2 pieces machine matzah, crumbled (not ground)
1 cup water
1 small onion, diced
2 tablespoons oil
2 eggs
2 sprigs fresh parsley, chopped,
    or 1 teaspoon dried parsley
4 tablespoons regular matzah meal
Pinch of salt and pepper

 Meat (in chicken soup)

 Makes about 10 balls

And here's how you do it!

1   Soak the crumbled matzah in cold water for a few minutes. Squeeze it out and set aside.

2   Sauté the onion in the oil over a medium flame until soft and light brown.

3   Beat the eggs with a fork and add this, together with the onions, to the matzah mush. Chop the fresh parsley and add it in as well. Sprinkle in the salt, pepper and matzah meal.

4   Mix the entire mixture together and refrigerate in a covered container for at least an hour.

5   Prepare a large pot of boiling salted water following the instructions on page 9 for Traditional Fluffy Matzah Balls. Wet your hands with water and form small balls, dropping them gently into the boiling water. Cook the matzah balls for 40 minutes.

6   Remove them with a slotted spoon; place on a flat plate and allow to cool.

These may now be frozen in plastic bags and removed for use as needed. What's especially nice about this recipe is how different it looks than the first matzah ball recipe.

Matzah Soup Squares

Do you like to do things that are not so typical?
Try this for a different twist on knaidelach!

Let's get to it!

3 eggs, beaten
¾ cup matzah meal
3 tablespoons water
3 tablespoons seltzer
¼ cup oil
½ teaspoon parsley flakes, optional
pinch of salt and pepper

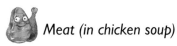 Meat (in chicken soup)

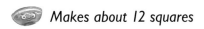 Makes about 12 squares

And here's how you do it!

1 Using a fork, beat the eggs for a few minutes. Add the matzah meal, water, seltzer, oil, parsley flakes, salt and pepper. Mix it all together with a fork.

2 Cover the bowl and put it in the refrigerator for at least an hour. After the batter has chilled, take out several square or rectangular-shaped ice cube molds. (A mold usually has spaces for 12 cubes.)

3 Roll a tablespoon of the batter in your wet fingers and then place some of the mixture into each cube. Gently press it down into the square space. Tap the ice cube mold on your working surface to release all the air pockets; add a bit more batter to each square and tap it again. This should settle the batter into each ice cube space pretty evenly. Freeze the molds.

4 Once they are frozen solid, boil up a large pot of salted water. When the water is boiling rapidly, pop the matzah ball squares out of the molds onto a plate and have an adult add them to the hot water. If for whatever reason your squares don't pop out, just run the underside of the mold under running sink water for a few seconds. Then they will pop out without any problem!

5 Cook them for 45 minutes. Remove your squares from the water with a slotted spoon and drain them.

Sometimes the "squares" are not quite as square after they have cooked. Even if this happens, they'll still be delicious, so don't sweat it! Mine came out a cute rectangular shape and we all enjoyed!

Miniature Charoses Balls

Here's a great new twist on charoses — make them into tiny balls, freeze, and enjoy for a snack or dessert any time on Passover!

Let's get to it!

1½ cups (200 grams) dried dates, pitted
and checked for bugs
½ cup (40–50 grams) yellow raisins
¾ cup (100 grams) dried apricots
1 green apple, peeled and ground
3 tablespoons semi-dry red wine
1 teaspoon cinnamon

 Pareve

 Makes 40–50 balls

Topping:
1 cup finely ground walnuts
½ cup finely shredded coconut, optional

And here's how you do it!

1 Place all dried fruits into a food processor that has been fitted with the "S" blade. Add the green apple, wine and cinnamon.

2 Turn on the food processor and puree it all together; you will need to stop and scrape down the fruit mix from the sides of the processor as necessary and then re-blend it.

3 Scrape the blended mixture into a plastic container and refrigerate until it is firm enough to roll into balls. (You may also freeze it for an hour so that it will become firm faster.)

To create the miniature balls:

1 Remove just a small amount of the mixture from the freezer at a time so the rest stays firm, and roll it into bite-sized balls.

2 Roll these balls into the finely ground nuts to coat them. You can roll some in ground nuts and some in ground coconut for a prettier look.

3 Place each one on a baking pan lined with parchment paper or directly into tiny decorative muffin liners. Once they are all rolled and coated, slide them back into the freezer until ready to use.

These look especially nice if you put a decorated toothpick into each ball before serving. You can buy them at any party goods store.

Fun Finger Foods

Fun Kids' Plate Idea

I make these adorable plates for my kids and any kid guests we sometimes have on Shabbos and holidays — everyone loves it and it's a great way for a little child to have something that will keep him at the table for at least 10 minutes!

Let's get to it!

Flat plates for each child
Lettuce leaves
Sliced cucumbers
One crunchy snack, such as potato chips
Dried fruit, such as mango, dates, or dried apricots
Jellybeans or another soft, colorful candy
A few chocolate chips
Marshmallows

 Pareve

And here's how you do it!

1 Line up the plates in front of you. Put one lettuce leaf off to one side of each plate, and a few slices of cucumber on the lettuce.

2 Put a handful of chips next to the lettuce. It is not necessary to put a lot on the plate in order to make it nice — a small amount of each thing is best.

3 Near the chips put a piece of whichever dried fruit or fruits you have. Add three jellybeans and four chocolate chips. Put one or two soft marshmallows in the center of the plate and serve.

Watch all the younger kids come running to see their nice plates instead of the "boring" fish and salad plates all the adults will be using ...

Turkey Shishkabobs

A quick and easy way to impress your guest or friend — and best of all, no cooking or roasting necessary!

Let's get to it!

4 wooden skewers
6 slices of turkey cold cuts
2 pickles
½ of a red pepper
½ of a yellow pepper
I fat rib of celery
I small cucumber
4 green olives
4 black olives
4 cherry tomatoes

 Meat

 Serves 2

And here's how you do it!

1 Take out all the ingredients so they are all ready. Place the skewers down in front of you on the table or your work surface.

2 Cut each cold cut slice into three strips. Roll each strip up, one at a time.

3 Cut each pickle into 6–8 chunks. Cut each pepper half into 6 chunks. Cut the rib of celery into 4 chunks. Cut the cucumber into 6 thick circles. (Leave the cherry tomatoes for later.)

4 Start to thread the different items onto the skewers. (But not the cherry tomatoes yet!)

5 First spear one of your turkey "rolls" and push it towards the bottom. Then add a pickle, a pepper, a cucumber circle, a celery chunk, another pickle, another turkey "roll," another pepper, an olive, a cucumber and so on, until you have all four skewers filled with yummy food. Each skewer will have between 4–5 cold cut "rolls" as well as bunches of veggies. Top each skewer's pointy end with a cherry tomato.

Put your turkey shishkabobs on a nice platter and serve. If you're preparing this in advance, cover the platter with plastic wrap and refrigerate until your guests arrive.

Roasted Shishkabobs

One of our favorite side dishes …

Let's get to it!

4 skewers
2 raw chicken cutlets
1 onion
1 zucchini
1 red pepper
1 small sweet potato

 Meat

 Serves 4

Seasoned Oil Sauce ingredients:
¼ cup olive oil
1 teaspoon garlic powder
1 teaspoon onion powder
1 teaspoon paprika
⅛ teaspoon pepper

And here's how you do it!

1 Place the skewers in front of you on the counter or your work surface.

2 Cut each chicken cutlet into about 12 bite-sized pieces. (Tip: raw cutlets slice best while they are still partially frozen.)

3 Cut off the skin and the first layer of the onion. Rinse it off and cut into small-size chunks. Wash the zucchini and pepper and cut into chunks. Scrub the sweet potato and cut into very small chunks. (Smaller-sized chunks of any kind of potato will roast faster.)

4 Mix the sauce ingredients in a small bowl and set aside.

5 Thread the different pieces onto the skewers. Make a pattern of chicken chunks, a piece of onion, pepper, more chicken, sweet potato, zucchini, onion, more chicken and so on until all the skewers are loaded with many chunks.

6 Line a 9x13-inch roasting or disposable baking pan with parchment paper. Place the skewers into the roasting pan. Using a brush, brush all your shishkabobs with the seasoned oil sauce you made.

7 Preheat the oven to 400°F (200°C). Roast the skewers for 10–15 minutes until the chicken pieces are cooked through.

15

Crispy Potato Shishkabobs

This is a great side dish for any barbecue and it takes much less time to roast than whole potatoes wrapped in foil …

Let's get to it!

4 skewers
1 large sweet potato or 2 small ones
2 medium-sized regular potatoes
A small bunch of very tiny onions
   or 1 regular onion
About ¼ cup oil or oil spray
Paprika
Onion powder

 Pareve

 Serves 4

And here's how you do it!

1 Scrub the sweet potatoes and potatoes well. Cut the sweet potatoes and regular potatoes into very small squares. It should make lots and lots of squares when it's cut so small!

2 Cut off the onion skin and the first layer. Rinse. Peel and rinse onions or, if you're using a whole onion, slice it in half, rinse it off, and cut it into smaller chunks.

3 Take out the skewers and thread the chunks of sweet potatoes, potatoes and onions onto them until they are very full. Place the skewers into a 9x13-inch disposable foil pan.

4 Smear the potatoes or spray them with cooking oil spray. Sprinkle them with the paprika and onion powder.

5 Preheat the oven to 400°F (200°C) and roast the skewers for 20 minutes.

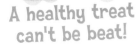
A healthy treat can't be beat!

Dried Fruit Kabobs

Another no-cook, no-roast, immediate-eat kind of food; and best of all, it's tasty, pretty and fun to eat. Sometimes we make these as small presents. We wrap each one in a piece of cellophane, tie a small ribbon near its bottom point, and welcome our guests by putting them in their glasses or on their nightstand.

Let's get to it!

4 skewers
4 dried apricots
4 dried dates
4 pitted prunes
I handful dried cranberries
I piece dried mango
I chunk dried papaya
I large circle dried pineapple
I piece fruit leather
2 circles dried apple

 Pareve

 Serves 4

And here's how you do it!

1 Place the skewers in front of you on the kitchen table.

2 Make sure all the dried fruit has been checked for bugs.

3 Open each apricot and tear it into two circles. Open each date, take out the pits, and pull each one apart so you have two pieces.

4 Cut the mango, pineapple and dried apple into four pieces each, or more if you prefer.

5 Thread the dried fruits onto the skewers in fun and colorful patterns, alternating the cranberries with the other dried fruits. End each one off with a piece of fruit leather folded into a square.

Candy-Stick Kabobs

My kids just LOVE it when I make them one of these as a holiday treat. You can use them as a sweet way to say "happy holiday" to any friend or visiting cousins or guests …

Let's get to it!

4 skewers
Piece of fruit leather that you can tear
   into four pieces
8 marshmallows
8 soft gummy candies of any kind
4 soft small taffies in several colors
8 jellybeans
4 mini-marshmallows

 Pareve

 Serves 4

And here's how you do it …

1 Place the skewers and the candies on the table in front of you.

2 Cut the fruit leather into four pieces and roll each one up so it sort of resembles a closed rose. Poke this onto the skewer and let it be the bottom-most piece.

3 Begin by pushing a marshmallow onto each skewer and pushing it down until a bit above the "rose" you just created.

4 Continue by adding pieces of taffy, gummy candies, the second big marshmallow and jellybeans in whatever pattern you like. Add the mini-marshmallow near the top so the sharp point is covered by something soft.

5 Wrap each skewer in a small piece of cellophane and close it with a ribbon. Using the flat side of the scissors blade, hold the loose parts of the tied ribbon against the scissors and then quickly pull the scissors down it. When you release it, the ribbon will jump back, curled nicely.

Present these to your friends or guests either in their glasses at the table or when they come to your door, as a sort of "flower." Watch their delighted expression of happiness!

Munch -a- Brunch

Matzah Brie

This is a traditional Passover breakfast or light lunch treat, easy to make and easy to eat …

Let's get to it!

5 eggs
½ cup milk
3 square matzahs
1 tablespoon butter

 Dairy

 Serves 4

And here's how you do it

1 Crack open eggs and put into a large bowl. Beat with a fork until they are a bit fluffy.

2 Crush the matzahs into bite-sized pieces and lay them down in another bowl; pour the milk over the matzah to soften it a bit.

3 Place a frying pan on the burner and set the flame to medium. Add the butter to the frying pan and let it melt while on the flame.

4 In the meantime, pour the eggs into the matzah and mix it with a fork. Add this to your hot pan and fry on both sides until it is cooked through, about 5 minutes. Keep stirring it and break it into many pieces while it is cooking, so that you will have many pieces of matzah brie.

Serve on four plates and top with cinnamon and sugar, and maybe a bit more butter for those who want it. Cream cheese or fruit jam is also great on top of your matzah brie.

Spicy Matzah Brie

Let's get to it!

Use the ingredients from the matzah brie on the previous page.
Add in:
½ teaspoon oregano
⅛ teaspoon pepper
1 teaspoon garlic powder
3 tablespoons ketchup or tomato sauce
½ cup shredded yellow cheese

 Dairy

 Serves 4

And here's how you do it!

1 Follow the directions for the first matzah brie. After putting the eggs into the softened matzahs, add the oregano, pepper, garlic powder, tomato sauce and yellow cheese.
Stir it together.

2 Heat the pan and add all the ingredients.

3 While it is cooking, continue to break it up a bit with your spatula and move it around and flip it a few times.

Mmm ... Doesn't the kitchen smell heavenly?

Scribbled Eggs

Now, many of know how to make an average egg. But this one's a little bit different and a lot tastier — impress your parents and friends!

Let's get to it!

5 large eggs
¼ cup cottage cheese
2 tablespoons milk
¼ teaspoon salt, optional
¼ teaspoon garlic powder
¼ teaspoon onion powder
1 slice American cheese

 Dairy

 Serves 3–4

And here's how you do it

1 Crack open eggs and put into a large bowl.

2 Add the cottage cheese, milk, salt, garlic powder, and onion powder. Stir it all together vigorously (that means really well!) with a fork. It should bubble up a bit.

3 Spray a frying pan with cooking oil spray. Place the pan on a medium-sized flame.

4 Add your eggs to the hot pan. Immediately pull off pieces of American cheese and add it to the eggs.

5 Using a wooden spatula, scribble the eggs in the pan, just like you'd scribble on a paper! The eggs should get cooked through in just a few minutes.

6 Turn off the flame so the eggs don't overcook and get hard.

Scoop your scribbled eggs onto three or four plates, or onto some waiting matzah pieces, and enjoy.

Matzah Marshmallow Melt

It's hard to believe that matzah can make something so yummy it could be a dessert!

Let's get to it!

- 4 square matzahs
- 4 tablespoons butter
- 2 cups mini-marshmallows
- I cup chocolate chips
- Cooking oil spray

 Dairy

 Serves 2

And here's how you do it!

1. Take the butter out of the fridge to soften it about a half hour before you plan to use it. Preheat the oven by turning it on to 350°F (180°C).

2. Spread butter on each piece of matzah. Line a dairy baking pan with parchment paper and place two of the buttered matzah pieces on it. The buttered side should be facing up.

3. Sprinkle I cup of mini-marshmallows onto each matzah. They should stick somewhat to the butter. If it does not stick, place the marshmallows on the matzah pieces one at a time and they will stick.

4. Sprinkle some chocolate chips in between the marshmallows.

5. Top with the second buttered matzah, with the buttered side facing down. Spray the top of the matzah melt with a bit of cooking oil spray.

6. Place pan in the hot oven for about 10 minutes, so that the marshmallows and chocolate chips melt. Use a spatula to flatten the matzahs together and then transfer the melts onto two plates.

Let it cool off a bit first and then enjoy! Just watch out — it's sure to make a sticky, yummy mess!

Cheesy Matzah Pie

Let's get to it!

6–7 square matzahs
5 eggs
1 cup milk
2 cups cottage cheese
⅓ cup sugar
¾ teaspoon salt
3 tablespoons butter, melted
1 teaspoon cinnamon

 Dairy

 Serves 6

And here's how you do it!

1 Beat the eggs and milk together in a bowl.

2 Add the cottage cheese, sugar, salt and melted butter. Mix again.

3 Grease a 2-quart casserole or baking dish. Preheat the oven to 350°F (180°C).

4 Break the matzahs into medium-sized pieces. Arrange part of them in one flat layer on the bottom of the baking dish.

5 Pour some of the cottage cheese mixture over the matzah. Place the rest of the matzah pieces on top and then pour the rest of the cottage cheese mix over the matzah. Depending on the size of your baking dish, you may have enough matzah pieces and cheese mix for either two or three layers. The top layer should be the cheese mixture.

6 Sprinkle cinnamon all over the top of the "pie."

7 Slide your matzah pie into the hot oven and let it bake for 35-40 minutes, until it is set.

Serve as is, or topped with sliced peaches or your favorite jam.

Matzah Pizza

This is a really easy one that we used to do all the time when we were kids …

Let's get to it!

4 slices matzah
1 cup tomato sauce
1 teaspoon oregano
1 teaspoon garlic powder
1 teaspoon onion powder
Pinch of black pepper, optional
2 cups shredded yellow cheese

 Dairy

 Serves 2

Additional toppings can include:
1 onion, chopped
Sliced green olives
Sliced mushrooms

And here's how you do it!

1 Preheat the oven to 350°F (180°C).

2 Line a dairy baking pan with parchment paper. Place the matzahs on the lined tray.

3 In a small bowl, mix together the tomato sauce, oregano, garlic powder, onion powder, and pepper. Spread some of this sauce all over the four matzahs. Top every matzah with the shredded yellow cheese.

4 If you like toppings, add the toppings of your choice to the matzahs.

5 Slide the baking pan into the hot oven and let it bake until the cheese is melted and bubbly, about 5 minutes.

Use a spatula to serve 2 slices of matzah pizza to you and your friend/ sister/ brother. Now make the milkshake on page 87 to go with it, and enjoy!

Blueberry Pancakes

This is a great and delicious recipe that anyone, any age, will certainly enjoy

Let's get to it!

3 eggs
¼ cup matzah meal
¾ cup cottage cheese
1 teaspoon sugar
½ teaspoon baking powder
1 teaspoon vanilla extract
1 tablespoon oil
½ cup fresh or frozen blueberries, rinsed and dried

 Dairy

 Serves 4

And here's how you do it ...

1 Crack open the eggs, put them into a large bowl and beat with a fork.

2 Add the matzah meal, cottage cheese, sugar, baking powder, vanilla extract and oil. Mix very well, until there are no lumps.

3 Dry the blueberries a bit with a paper towel. Add them to the batter.

4 Spray a frying pan with cooking oil spray and turn on a medium flame. When it's hot, pour 2 large spoonfuls of batter into the pan. When you see small bubbles forming on the pancake, flip it over and fry on the second side. When it's cooked through, remove from the pan and stack on a plate until they are all done.

Serve them as is, or with some butter on top, and enjoy!

For maximum pleasure, be sure to measure!

Blueberry or Peach Muffins

The last time I made these I thought I'd be generous and give a few to my neighbor to sample, but before I turned around, they were all eaten up…

Let's get to it!

4 large eggs
½ cup oil
I cup sugar
¾ cup matzah meal
¼ cup potato starch
¼ cup orange juice
I tablespoon vanilla sugar
½ teaspoon baking soda
¼ teaspoon baking powder
¾ cup frozen blueberries
   or 4 fresh or 6 canned peach halves, diced

Topping:
¼ cup sugar
4 teaspoons cinnamon

 Pareve

 Makes 12 muffins

And here's how you do it...

1 Preheat the oven to 350°F (180°C).

2 In a large bowl, beat the eggs with a hand blender until they are a bit fluffy. Add everything else except the blueberries. Mix until it is a smooth mixture.

3 Add half the blueberries and mix by hand. (If you use your hand mixer, the blueberries will be crushed.) The batter should now be a bit purple-ish. If you are using peaches instead, add them now.

4 Line a muffin tray with cupcake holders. Pour ¼ cup of the mixture into each one; they should be filled nearly to the top.

5 Place the remainder of the berries on top of each muffin. Push them down a bit so they are mostly covered by batter.

6 Mix the topping ingredients with a spoon and sprinkle over the muffins.

7 Place the tray in the oven and bake for 15 minutes, until the muffins have puffed up and are baked through. Remove from the oven right away.

Great eaten as is or with a bit of cream cheese on top.

Matzah Meal Rolls

I have this great recipe from my mother, who got it from her friend Mrs. Faigy Males. My mother-in-law, Mrs. Gloria Ansh, has also been making matzah meal rolls like this for over 40 years …

Let's get to it!

2 cups matzah meal
1 teaspoon salt
1 tablespoon sugar
1 cup hot water
½ cup oil
4 eggs

 Pareve

 Makes 11–12 rolls

And here's how you do it …

1   Preheat the oven to 375°F (190°C). Put the matzah meal, salt and sugar in a bowl and mix together. Make a hole in the center of the mixture and add the hot water and oil.

2   Start to mix it together, adding the eggs one at a time. It should turn into a thick batter. (My mother says to let the batter stand for 15 minutes at this point, before forming the rolls. However, when I am in a rush I make it right after mixing and it works just fine.)

3   Line a cookie sheet with parchment paper. Spray the paper with a bit of cooking oil spray.

4   Wet your hands slightly and form small, oblong or round rolls. Place them on the baking tray, with a small amount of space between them. (These rolls are very similar in shape to regular matzah balls; the main difference is that these will be baked while matzah balls are boiled.)

5   Bake the rolls for 40–45 minutes until they are lightly browned on both the top and bottom. Remove from the pan to a wire rack to cool.

I always make the entire amount of this recipe because the rolls come out smallish and most people want to eat at least two! If you have any left over, they can be frozen and used the next day …

If you want ideas for how to stuff your rolls, try any of the following toppings, or just think of any other great ideas of your own — and you can always decide to just stick with ketchup and yellow cheese, melted in your roll in the oven …

Topping ideas:

Tuna Topping — Mash one can of tuna with one hard-boiled egg and 1–2 tablespoons mayo. Add some diced scallions and/or 1 stalk of diced celery, if you like.

Egg Topping — Mash 3 hard-boiled eggs with 2 tablespoons mayonnaise. Add about 1 tablespoon diced onions and a pinch of pepper.

Cheese Topping — Mix ½ cup cream cheese with 1 tablespoon onion soup mix.

Garlic Topping — Mix ½ cup cream cheese with 1 tablespoon garlic powder and 1 teaspoon dried dill.

Avocado Topping — Mash 1 large, ripe avocado with ½ teaspoon lemon juice, 2 teaspoons garlic powder, 2 teaspoons onion powder, ½ teaspoon salt, and a very small amount of black pepper. If you like, you can add 2 hard-boiled eggs to this and mash it together.

Let's clean up!

Soups & Other Such Stuff

Pastel-Colored Soup

This soup freezes well.

Let's get to it!

2 tablespoons oil
1 large onion, diced
3 large, firm carrots, peeled
   and cut into chunks
3–4 medium-sized green zucchini,
   scrubbed and cut into chunks
1 potato, peeled and cut into chunks
1½ teaspoons salt
¼ teaspoon pepper

 Pareve

 Serves 4

And here's how you do it!

1 Take out a large soup pot. Turn on the fire. Add the oil, and fry the onion until it looks clear and light brown.

2 Add the chunks of carrots, zucchini and potato. Add enough water to cover all the vegetables, plus 3 more cups of water. Add the salt and pepper.

3 Heat the soup until it boils; turn the flame down to simmer and continue to cook for another hour. Turn off the flame.

4 Using a hand blender, puree the soup until it is completely smooth and creamy. The soup should now be a soft pastel orange color.

Chicken Soup

You can actually help prepare one of the main foods for the meal!

Let's get to it!

2 tablespoons oil
1 onion, diced
2 cloves garlic, diced
4–6 pieces of chicken parts,
    such as the wings and necks, rinsed off
Water
1 zucchini, scrubbed and cubed
2 carrots, sliced
1 small ripe tomato, halved
1 rib of celery, sliced
3 pieces fresh dill
3 pieces fresh parsley
2–3 teaspoons salt
¼ teaspoon pepper

 Meat

 Serves 6

And here's how you do it!

1 Put a 6–8 quart pot on the stovetop. Add the oil. Add the diced onion and garlic. Turn on the flame and fry the onion and garlic until they are light brown.

2 Turn the flame down a bit and add the chicken pieces. Stir with the onion/garlic pieces until brown on all sides. This should take five minutes.

3 Add enough water to reach halfway to the top of the pot. Add the zucchini, carrots, tomato halves, celery, dill, parsley, salt and pepper. Add more water, so the pot is filled close to the top but not all the way. There needs to be room for the soup to bubble without spilling over the sides of the pot.

4 Heat the soup until it boils. Once it is boiling, turn down the flame to simmer; keep the pot covered and let it cook for 2–3 hours.

Your house should smell amazing while it's cooking, and in no time at all, you will have your very own real chicken soup to serve to your whole family! (This freezes well.) Now go ahead and make some of those nifty matzah balls from the beginning of this book so you have something fun and delicious to add to your soup pot …

Thick 'n' Creamy Chicken Soup

Here's a really creative idea for a new twist on regular chicken soup!

Let's get to it!

One recipe of chicken soup from page 30
The carrots from that soup,
    already cooked
1 boiled potato
A bit of paprika for sprinkling later on

 Meat

 Serves 6

And here's how you do it!

1 Do this while the chicken soup is cool. Remove the carrots from the soup. Set them aside in a bowl together with the boiled potato.

2 Take all the chicken pieces out of the soup. Take all the chicken off the bones, and throw out the bones.

3 Put the cooked chicken pieces back into the pot. Using a hand blender, blend the soup together with all the veggies and cooked chicken pieces until it is thick, smooth and creamy.

4 Put the soup back onto the fire to simmer
while you finish the last step.

5 Take the cold carrots that you saved and cut them into tiny cubes.

6 To serve, spoon the soup into bowls. Add a few of the carrot cubes to the middle of each bowl, sprinkle it with a bit of paprika if you like for a pretty effect, and serve.

STOP! Don't put that pot down near the edge of the counter!

Potato Soup

We'll make this one dairy as a good opener for a lighter Passover meal …

Let's get to it!

2 tablespoons butter
2 onions, diced
4 large potatoes, peeled and cubed
Water to cover
2 teaspoons salt
¼ teaspoon pepper
1 cup milk
½ cup shredded yellow cheese

  Dairy

Serves 4

And here's how you do it!

1 Take out a large dairy soup pot. Add the butter and chopped onions. Ask an adult to turn on the flame, and fry the onions until they turn light brown. While they are frying, peel and cut the potatoes. Add them into the onion mixture.

2 Add enough water to cover all the potatoes, plus 3 more cups of water. Let it begin to boil. Add the salt and pepper while it is boiling up.

3 After it boils, cover the pot, turn the flame down and let the soup cook for 45 minutes to one hour, until all the potatoes are soft. Turn off the fire.

4 Using a handblender, puree the soup until it is smooth. Add the milk and puree again. It should thicken and combine together.

5 Heat the soup once more until it is warm and bubbly. After ladling some soup into a few bowls, add some shredded yellow cheese to the center of each soup bowl, and serve.

If you want a really fun color potato soup, try doing this: Substitute 3 sweet potatoes for 3 of the white potatoes in this recipe and use 1 white potato. Then you'll have orange-colored potato soup.

Another fun serving idea — if you make BOTH color soups, you can serve two-toned soup to your guests! Put both finished soups on the counter, and ask someone to help you. Each of you should use a ladle to pour some soup into the soup bowl at the same time, from two different sides of the bowl. This way your soup bowls will each be "two-toned" in color, one half of each bowl being white and one half the bowl orange. People will be amazed at how you did it!

Stuffed Matzah Balls

Surprise your family as they cut into these matzah balls …

Let's get to it!

I recipe of Traditional Fluffy Matzah Balls
   from the first recipe in this book, page 9
½ lb. (250 grams) ground meat
   or ground chicken
I cooked and mashed potato
I teaspoon salt

 Meat

 Serves many …

And here's how you do it!

1 Make one recipe of matzah ball batter. Put the mixture in the fridge for an hour until firm.

2 Mix the meat and the mashed potato together. This will be the "meat mixture."

3 Fill a large, wide pot ¾ full with water and add the salt. Turn on the flame and boil the water.

4 Form very small meatballs out of your meat mix. Lay them down on a plate so they are ready when you need them.

5 Dip your hands into water; take about a tablespoon of matzah ball batter and flatten into the cup of your hand. Put one meat "ball" into the middle of the batter in your hand. Add some more matzah meal batter over that meat "ball" so it is covered, and now roll it in your hand so it is a perfect ball.

6 Drop this gently into the boiling water and continue on to the next stuffed matzah ball, until you finish all the batter.

7 Boil the stuffed matzah balls for 45 minutes and then drain them and freeze for later use. Add them to boiling soup about 30–45 minutes before you want to serve them, and enjoy!

If you run out of meatballs, just make the rest into ordinary matzah balls.

If you run out of matzah ball batter, use the meatballs for regular meatballs.

Fish Your Own Fish

Really Easy Gefilte Fish

Making your own fish roll is so simple if you just know what to do with one of those great store-bought rolls!

Let's get to it!

1 frozen ready-made gefilte fish roll
1 onion
1 carrot
1 teaspoon salt
⅓ cup sugar
Water

 Pareve

 Serves 10

And here's how you do it ...

1 Take out a large pot and fill it halfway with water.

2 Peel the onion, cut it in half and rinse it off. Add this to the pot. Add the carrot, salt and sugar.

3 Turn on the flame, and heat this up until it boils. When the water is boiling, remove the roll of fish from the plastic outer wrapping. Put the fish in the pot while it is still wrapped in its inner wrapping (this is the parchment paper). Let the water boil again, and then cover the pot and lower the flame to simmer.

4 Simmer your fish on a medium-low flame for 1½ hours. When it's done, turn off the flame. Remove it from the pot to a plastic container together with the carrot, onion, and some of the broth. Refrigerate until use.

Serve sliced on a plate with a piece of carrot on top of each slice for decoration!

Moroccan-Style Gefilte Fish

Okay, so maybe this one is messing around with two different customs of fish — "gefilte fish" is mostly Eastern European, and Morrocan-style is mostly, well, Sefardi, but it comes out so good that I just had to share it ...

Let's get to it!

I frozen, ready-made gefilte fish roll
I cup tomato paste
I tablespoon olive oil
I tablespoon paprika
I teaspoon hot paprika (cayenne pepper)
I tablespoon garlic powder
I tablespoon onion powder
¼ teaspoon ground ginger
I onion, diced
I carrot, peeled and cut into round slices

 Pareve

 Serves 10

And here's how you do it!

1 Preheat the oven to 375°F (190°C).

2 Line a loaf pan with parchment paper. Peel off the wrapper and parchment paper from the frozen fish loaf and place it in the lined loaf pan.

3 In a small bowl, mix together the tomato paste, olive oil and all the spices.

4 Smear this all over the fish loaf and add in any leftover tomato paste.

5 Place the cut onions and carrots all over the fish loaf and in any spaces you find in the pan.

6 Cover the loaf with the parchment paper and then again with a piece of foil. Seal the edges well.

7 Bake for 1½ hours. Remove from the oven and let cool; refrigerate until serving.

Serve sliced, with the cooked veggies on the side. Really delish and quite different, too!

Cucumber Holders

Gefilte fish is almost always served with chrain (horseradish) and mayonnaise on the side. Here's a nifty little way to serve it!

Let's get to it!

4 small, fat, firm cucumbers
Red chrain (horseradish)
Mayonnaise
Dried dill, optional
4 crunchy lettuce leaves
8 cherry tomatoes
Melon baller

 Pareve

 Serves 4

And here's how you do it ...

1 Wash off each cucumber and cut each one into two halves the fat way, not the long way.

2 Using the melon baller, scoop out most of the inside of each cuke. Be careful not to scoop all the way to the bottom of the cuke. Set the cucumber balls aside for later.

3 Take out four plates. Slice off the bottom of each holed-out cucumber so it will stand up on the plate. Be careful not to slice too much; you don't want to slice all the way until your hole.

4 Put two cucumber holders onto each plate with the hole side facing upwards.

5 Spoon some chrain into one cucumber holder and some mayonnaise into the other cucumber holder. If you like, sprinkle some dill onto the mayonnaise one; it will look fancy!

6 Put the two cucumber balls onto each plate, with two cherry tomatoes.

7 Lay the lettuce leaf in the center of the plate. Place a slice of fish on the lettuce. Top with a slice of carrot and serve. It will look like a caterer prepared this dish!

Nova Finger Treats

This is fancy enough to impress VIP guests!

Let's get to it!

1 package of Nova/smoked salmon/a.k.a. lox
1 small container of cream cheese
Tiny cherry tomatoes, about 10
Green olives without pits
10–15 matzah crackers
1 medium cucumber, washed and sliced
Toothpicks

 Dairy

 Serves 2

And here's how you do it!

1 Prepare a nice serving platter.

2 Cut the lox into thin strips. Roll up each strip so it looks like a mini jelly roll.

3 Smear a little cream cheese onto each cracker.
It won't smear onto the cuke slices so just put small dollops on each one with a spoon. You can get creative by putting the cream cheese in a piping bag with a large star tip at the end, and swirling the cream cheese onto each cracker and cuke slice.

4 Top each one with a lox roll.

5 Pierce one cherry tomato or one green olive with a toothpick, then poke the end into the Nova treats. Put them all on a platter and serve.

Please don't forget to put us away when you're done ...

Salmon Latkes

Let's get to it!

- 1 15 oz. can (or about 450 grams) of salmon, drained and flaked
- 2 eggs
- ¼ cup matzah meal
- ¼ cup dried potato flakes
- 1 medium onion, diced
- 1 clove garlic, diced
- ¼ teaspoon dill
- ½ teaspoon garlic powder
- ½ teaspoon onion powder
- Pinch of pepper
- 2–3 tablespoons oil

 Pareve

 Serves 4

And here's how you do it!

1. Open the can of salmon. Drain and empty into a large bowl. Remove all the skin and bones.

2. Add everything else except the oil and mix together. Add the oil to the frying pan.

3. Turn on the flame. Make small balls out of the mix and place in the frying pan. Flatten them with the back of a spatula when they are in the pan. Fry the salmon latkes on both sides.

Serve over a bed of lettuce, with sliced tomatoes and green olives on the side.

Whee! What fun!

Instant Tasty Salmon Steaks

Let's get to it!

4 salmon steaks, rinsed
   and patted dry with paper towels
¼ cup mayonnaise
1 tablespoon onion soup mix
2 tablespoons paprika
½ tablespoon garlic powder
¼ teaspoon pepper
½ teaspoon dried dill

 Pareve

 Serves 4

And here's how you do it!

1 Preheat the oven to 400°F (200°C).

2 Place the salmon steaks on a baking pan that is lined
   with parchment paper.

3 In a small bowl, mix the mayo, soup mix, and spices.

4 Spread this mixture all over the top of each salmon steak.

5 Slide them into the oven and let it bake for 20 minutes.

6 Test the center of one of the steaks with a fork. If it flakes and is
   cooked through, it's done.

7 Take the steaks out of the oven immediately.

Serve and enjoy!

Meat
and
Chicken

Meat Burgers

Let's get to it!

1 lb. (450 grams) ground meat,
  turkey or chicken
1 onion, pureed or diced
1 carrot, pureed, optional
2 eggs
¼ cup matzah meal
¼ teaspoon pepper
1 teaspoon garlic powder

 Meat

 Serves 4

And here's how you do it!

1 Open the meat package and empty it into a bowl. Mash it a bit with a fork to separate the pieces.

2 Add everything else and mix it with a fork.

3 Form flat patties out of the meat mixture.

4 Spray a large frying pan with cooking oil spray and heat it on the flame. Cook the meat burgers on both sides until browned.

5 Serve and enjoy with mashed potatoes or a salad.

You can use the Matzah Rolls as buns for these burgers.

Easy Sauce Chicken

Let's get to it!

4 chicken legs, each cut in half so you
   have 4 thighs and 4 drumsticks
1 onion, sliced
½ cup mayonnaise
¼ cup apricot jam
3 tablespoons onion soup mix
1 cup ketchup
Paprika

 Meat

 Serves 4–5

And here's how you do it!

1 Preheat the over to 375°F (190°C).

2 Place the chicken pieces into the roasting pan. Pat them dry with a paper towel. Throw out the paper towel when you are done.

3 In a bowl, mix the mayo, apricot jam, onion soup mix and ketchup. Smear this mix underneath the skin of all the chicken pieces; smear the top of each piece with the remaining mixture.

4 Sprinkle paprika on each piece of chicken. Lay the onion slices on top of all the pieces of chicken.

5 Cover the pan with parchment paper and then foil. Slide it into the hot oven and bake it for 45 minutes.

6 Uncover the chicken and baste it a bit. Return it to the oven and bake for another 20 minutes, uncovered.

7 Remove from the oven right away so it won't dry out.

Be sure to wipe up
any spills ...

Coated Chicken Shake

Even picky eaters will like this recipe ...

Let's get to it!

1 chicken, skins removed, cut into serving pieces
1½ cups matzah meal
¼ teaspoon pepper
1 tablespoon parsley flakes
2 teaspoons oregano
1 tablespoon garlic powder
1 tablespoon onion powder
2 eggs
1 onion, sliced

 Meat

 Serves 5–6

And here's how you do it!

1 Preheat the oven to 375°F (190°C).

2 Spray baking pan with cooking oil spray and layer the onions on the bottom of the pan.

3 Put the matzah meal into a large bowl. Add all the spices and mix.

4 Crack open the eggs and add them to a different bowl; beat the eggs with a fork.

5 Dip each chicken piece into the matzah meal bowl. Then dip it into the egg bowl and once again into the matzah meal bowl.

6 As you are finished dipping the piece of chicken, place each one into the baking pan. When all the pieces are done, spray the tops of the coated chicken with cooking oil spray.

7 Bake uncovered for 1 hour.

Heat up ½ cup apricot jam in a small pot until it is liquidy. After all the chicken pieces are lined up in the pan, drizzle some of this melted apricot jam over them all. Then slide the pan into the oven. You can bake the chicken covered by putting parchment paper over it and then foil, or uncovered as instructed above. Both ways are superb.

If you are baking the chicken uncovered, you should check it after 40 minutes of baking time to make sure it is not getting burned or dried out. If it is, cover it until it finishes cooking.

Crunchy Chicken Crisps

My kids have friends who make chicken like this and have been asking me for ages to do it with them too. What a treat!

Let's get to it!

4 chicken legs, each cut in half so you
   have 4 drumsticks and 4 thighs
½ cup matzah meal or potato starch
I tablespoon garlic powder
I tablespoon onion powder
¼ teaspoon black pepper
I tablespoon paprika
I teaspoon parsley flakes
I large bag potato chips (200-gram bag)
4 eggs
Cooking oil spray

 Meat

 Serves 4

And here's how you do it!

1 Wash off the chicken legs; take the skin off each one. Pat them dry and place them on a plate. Preheat the oven to 375°F (190°C).

2 Place the matzah meal (or potato starch) and all the spices into a bowl. Mix together with a fork.

3 Put all the eggs into another bowl, and beat them lightly with a fork.

4 In another bowl, crush the potato chips into very small pieces.

5 Spray a large baking pan with cooking oil spray. Dip each chicken piece into the matzah meal mix with the spices, then the egg, and then the potato chips. Lay it down in the pan and continue until all the chicken pieces have been double-coated.

6 Any matzah meal crumbs and/or potato chip crumbs that are left over must be thrown out. They had raw chicken dipped into them and cannot be eaten! Don't lick your fingers after dipping them into the potato chip crumbs. Wash your hands off really well after handling raw chicken.

7 Spray the chicken pieces with the cooking oil spray to coat. Slide the pan into the oven and bake for 50–60 minutes until the chicken is fork-tender. Do not overbake.

Really Good, Quick Meatballs in Sauce

Always a favorite …

Let's get to it!

1 lb. (450 grams) ground turkey
   or chicken
1 lb. (450 grams) ground meat,
   or more turkey if you prefer
2 eggs
½ cup matzah meal
2 medium-sized onions, pureed
2 cloves garlic, pureed, optional
1 cup tomato paste
1 cup water
1 cup ketchup
4 tablespoons regular or dark sugar
2 tablespoons vinegar or lemon juice
1½ teaspoons salt
¼ teaspoon pepper
1 sliced onion

 Meat

 Serves 6

And here's how you do it!

1 Place the ground meats, eggs, matzah meal, and pureed onions and garlic into a large bowl. Mix together.

2 Cover the bowl and place the meat mixture into the fridge to firm up a bit while you make the sauce.

3 In a large, deep and wide pot, add the tomato paste, water, ketchup, sugar, vinegar (or lemon juice) and salt. Turn on the flame. Let the sauce start to bubble and cook, and then turn down flame to simmer. Add the sliced onion.

4 Remove the meat mixture from the fridge and form it into small balls. Drop them into the bubbling sauce.

5 Close the lid and let it cook for an hour.

Serve over steamed or boiled potato chunks or mashed potatoes.

Meatloaf

Let's get to it!

1 lb. (450 grams) ground chicken or meat
2 eggs
½ teaspoon salt
¼ teaspoons pepper
1 teaspoon garlic powder
1 tablespoon onion soup mix
¼ cup ketchup
½ cup matzah meal
1 onion
1 carrot
1 potato
1 stalk celery
2 teaspoons paprika

 Meat

 Serves 2–3

And here's how you do it!

1 Preheat the oven to 350°F (180°C).

2 Put the ground meat in a bowl.

3 Add the eggs, salt, pepper, garlic powder, onion soup mix, ketchup, and matzah meal. Mix.

4 Put the onion, carrot, potato and celery into the food processor. Puree them all.

5 Add the pureed veggies to the meat mix. Combine.

6 Line a loaf pan with parchment paper. Pour the meat mixture into the pan, and pat it down into a loaf shape. Sprinkle the top with paprika.

7 Bake for 35–40 minutes until done. Serve hot.

Crispy Chicken Cutlets (CCC's)

Triple delicious!!!

Let's get to it!

4 smaller chicken cutlets,
  washed and dried off
2 eggs
1 cup matzah meal
3 teaspoons garlic powder
2 teaspoons onion powder
¼ teaspoon pepper
½ teaspoon oregano
1 teaspoon dried parsley
3–4 tablespoons oil

 Meat

 Serves 2

And here's how you do it!

1 Put the eggs into one bowl. Beat lightly.

2 Put the matzah meal and all the spices into a second bowl and toss them together.

3 Slice each cutlet in half, so they will be more kid-friendly in size. Dip each cutlet into the matzah meal, then the egg, and again into the matzah meal.

4 Put a large frying pan on the stove and turn on the flame. Add some of the oil as the pan starts to heat up.

5 Place the coated cutlets into the pan and begin to cook them on a medium flame. When they are crispy and golden on the first side, after about 10 minutes of cooking time, turn them over to cook on the second side. You may need to add a bit more oil.

6 They are ready when they are crispy on both sides and cooked through, about 15–20 minutes total.

7 Thicker pieces of cutlets take a bit longer; thinner pieces cook faster. Remove the cutlets as soon as they are done; do not overcook them or they will be dry.

Serve your CCC's on nice plates and cut right in!

Spicy Chicken Bake

Let's get to it!

- 1 whole chicken, cut into eighths
- 2 onions, sliced
- 1 large sweet potato, chopped
- 2 cups frozen baby carrots
- 1 tablespoon garlic powder
- 1 tablespoon onion powder
- ¼ teaspoon pepper
- 1 tablespoon paprika
- 1 teaspoon ginger
- Cooking oil spray

 Meat

 Serves 4

And here's how to do it!

1 Preheat the oven to 375°F (190°C).

2 Place the chicken pieces in a baking pan. Put the sweet potato chunks and carrots in between or underneath the chicken pieces.

3 Mix the spices together in a small bowl. Sprinkle some of the spice mixture underneath the skin of the chicken pieces. Sprinkle the rest of the spice mixture on top of the chicken pieces.

4 Lightly spray the spiced chicken with cooking oil spray. Place the onion slices on top of the chicken.

5 Cover the pan with parchment paper and then with aluminum foil.

6 Place the pan in the hot oven and bake for 1 hour and 10 minutes.

Serve hot.

Oooh ... yummy!

Barbecue-Flavored Chicken Wings

Great (but sticky) finger food!

Let's get to it!

1 large onion, cut into rings
16–20 chicken wings, cleaned
½ cup honey
½ cup ketchup
½ cup apricot jam
2 tablespoons oil
1 tablespoon garlic powder
1 tablespoon onion powder
2 teaspoons ginger

 Meat

 Serves 5–6

And here's how you do it!

1 Preheat the oven to 375°F (190°C).

2 Layer the onion rings on the bottom of a pan. Place the chicken wings on top of the onion rings.

3 In a bowl, mix the honey, ketchup, jam, oil and spices.

4 Smear this mixture all over the wings.

5 Slide the pan into the oven and roast for 25–35 minutes, until the wings are cooked.

Surprise Matzah Meatballs in Sauce

Let's get to it!

One recipe of Stuffed Matzah Balls from page 33
1 onion
2 cloves garlic
2 tablespoons oil
2 cups tomato paste
2 cups water
2–3 teaspoons salt
½ teaspoon pepper
4 tablespoons sugar
1 tablespoon lemon juice

 Meat

 Serves 4–6

And here's how you do it!

1 Slice the onion and cut the garlic into very small pieces. Add them to a large pot with the oil and turn on the flame so they will start sizzling.

2 Add the tomato paste, and then fill up the empty can with water twice and add that to the pot. Stir it together so it forms a sort of soup.

3 Add the salt, pepper, sugar and lemon juice. When the sauce starts to bubble, stir it and then turn the flame down as low as possible. Cover the pot.

4 Add the "stuffed matzah balls" to the pot. Add any meatballs you also made from the leftover ground meat.

5 Cover the pot and let it cook for 1 hour.

Serve hot over mashed potatoes and enjoy!

49

Veggies, Salads and Potatoes

Israeli Salad

Let's get to it!

- 3 cucumbers
- 2 firm tomatoes
- I red pepper
- ½ a small onion or I scallion
- I pickle
- ½ teaspoon salt
- ⅛ teaspoon pepper
- I teaspoon garlic powder
- 3 teaspoons oil

Pareve

Serves 2–3

And here's how you do it!

1. Cut all the veggies into very small pieces and put them into a bowl.
2. Add all the spices. Pour in the oil.
3. Mix the salad very well with a large spoon.

Cucumber Salad

Let's get to it!

6 regular-sized cucumbers
1 teaspoon salt
6 tablespoons sugar
¼ teaspoon pepper
¼ cup vinegar
1 small onion, either white or purple

 Pareve

 Serves 4

And here's how you do it!

1 Peel all the cucumbers and rinse them off.

2 Cut them into very thin rounds or slice them in a food processor.

3 Place the cut cukes into a large bowl. Sprinkle with salt and toss.

4 Add the sugar, pepper and vinegar.

5 Slice the onion into half rounds and add it to the bowl. Toss together and refrigerate for a few hours before serving.

No ... don't sneeze NOW!

Coleslaw

Let's get to it!

1 bag shredded green cabbage
2 carrots
¾ cup sugar
½ cup vinegar
1 teaspoon salt
½ teaspoon pepper
½ cup mayonnaise

 Pareve

 Serves 4

And here's how you do it!

1 Empty the cabbage into a bowl. Shred the carrots in a food processor and add them to the bowl.

2 Add the sugar, vinegar, salt and pepper. Mix it all together.

3 Add the mayonnaise and mix.

4 Put your coleslaw into a plastic container and refrigerate until serving.

To make your coleslaw multi-colored, instead of one whole bag of green cabbage, use half a bag of green and half a bag of purple cabbage. You'll love the colors!

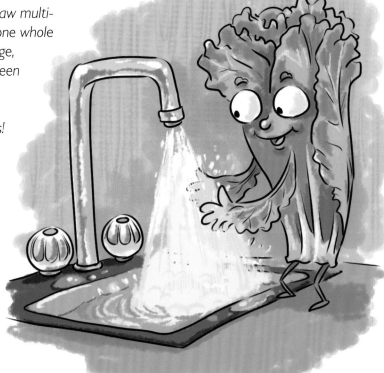

Wash your hands before you start!

Fruity Beet Salad

Let's get to it!

3 medium-sized fresh beets
2 canned peach halves
1 ripe pear, cut into small chunks
¼ cup golden raisins
½ of a very small red onion, sliced
½ cup orange juice

 Pareve

 Serves 4

And here's how you do it!

1 Peel and cut every beet into four pieces. Place them in a pot and cover them with water. Turn on the flame. Boil them for 40 minutes until they are soft. Allow to cool.

2 Shred the beets in the food processor. Drain off most, but not all, of their juice. Add the rest of the ingredients and mix together.

3 Refrigerate for several hours before serving.

Beets shred better when they have first been refrigerated several hours or overnight, after being cooked. Also, it's a very good idea to wear disposable gloves and an apron when working with beets — they stain quite a bit!

French Fries

Let's get to it!

6 potatoes
2 teaspoons garlic powder
2 teaspoons paprika
¼ cup oil

 Pareve

 Serves 4

And here's how you do it!

1 Peel the potatoes and rinse them off.

2 Slice the potatoes into long sticks so they look like fries. Place them into a bowl.

3 Add the spices and oil and toss together.

4 Line a baking pan with parchment paper.

5 Spread the fries out onto the parchment paper in one layer.

6 Bake them at 400°F (200°C) until they are crispy and crunchy, about 45 minutes.

Enjoy with ketchup or salt.

Make 'em Spicy Fries! Just add ¼ teaspoon black pepper and 1 teaspoon hot paprika or cayenne pepper to the fries when you are tossing them. Then bake them and see what happens …

STOP! Check that no one small is nearby when you open the oven door …

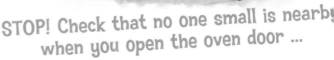

Veggie Kabobs

Let's get to it!

1 cucumber
6 cherry tomatoes
1 red pepper
1 yellow pepper
1 orange pepper
1 pickle
2 green olives
2 black olives
4 wooden skewers

  Pareve

 Serves 2

And here's how you do it!

1 Cut the cukes into fat rounds.

2 Cut the peppers into chunks or use a small flower cookie cutter to press out round flower shapes from the peppers. (The extra pepper pieces can be made into Israeli salad, see recipe on page 50.)

3 Cut the pickle into fat rounds.

4 On each skewer, thread the veggies in any order you like: a cuke round, several colorful pepper pieces, a cherry tomato, a pickle, and then begin your pattern again.

5 Top each one with an olive and then a cherry tomato on top of the point of the skewer.

6 Since you now have four veggie kabobs, you and your friend can each have two.

Make a simple dip to add zing — just mix 2 tablespoons of mayo with 2 tablespoons of ketchup and voila, you now have a dip!

Pizza Potatoes

This is filling enough to serve as a main dish

Let's get to it!

6 medium-sized potatoes
2 cups tomato sauce
1 teaspoon oregano
½ teaspoon salt
3 teaspoons garlic powder
1 teaspoon onion powder
1 cup shredded yellow cheese (like mozzarella)

 Dairy

 Serves 3–4

And here's how you do it!

1 Peel the potatoes. Put them in a pot and cover them with water. Ask an adult to turn on the flame and boil them for 30 minutes. Rinse the potatoes off in a colander so they will cool down faster.

2 Pour the tomato sauce into a small bowl and add all the spices. Mix with a spoon.

3 Slice the potatoes in thin rounds and layer in a glass baking dish. After you have one layer, spoon some sauce over them to cover, sprinkle a layer of cheese, and then add another layer of sliced potatoes.

4 Keep doing this until your dish is full. The last thing on top should be the cheese.

5 Cover the dish with the glass cover and bake at 350°F (180°C) for 45 minutes, until it is bubbly and cooked through. Serve immediately.

Potato Salad

Let's get to it!

4 boiled and cooled potatoes
2 dill pickles
1 stalk celery
½ small purple onion
2 hard-boiled eggs
1 carrot, shredded, optional
2 tablespoons mayonnaise
½ teaspoon salt
¼ teaspoon pepper

 Pareve

 Serves 4

And here's how you do it!

1 Cut the potatoes, pickles, celery, onion and eggs into small pieces.

2 Put them into a large bowl.

3 Add the shredded carrot.

4 Add the mayonnaise, salt and pepper.

5 Mix well and refrigerate.

6 Super yummy!

For a different sort of kick, cut up 3 slices of deli meat and add it to your potato salad. This will make the salad "meaty" but it will sure taste great!

Nothing like fresh horseradish for the Seder!

Sweet Potato Puffs

Let's get to it!

4 medium-sized sweet potatoes
3 tablespoons oil
½ teaspoon salt
⅛ teaspoon pepper
2 cups canned pineapple chunks, drained
⅔ cup matzah meal
   or finely ground walnuts or almond flour

 Pareve

 Makes about 20–24 balls

And here's how you do it!

1 Peel the sweet potatoes and cut into chunks. Put into a medium-sized pot and add water to cover the sweet potatoes. Turn on the flame and boil the sweet potatoes for about 40 minutes, until they are soft. Have an adult help you drain off the hot water.

2 Preheat the oven to 350°F (180°C).

3 Mash the sweet potatoes in a bowl with the salt, pepper and oil.

4 When it cools down enough to touch, form the mixture into small balls, pressing one pineapple chunk into the center of each one, and forming the ball around this chunk.

5 Roll each ball in matzah meal (or you can use the finely ground walnuts or almond flour instead).

6 Line a baking pan with parchment paper and spray with cooking oil spray. Place the sweet potato puffs on the tray. Spray the outside of each one with some cooking oil spray.

7 When the pan is full, slide it into the oven and bake for about 20 minutes or until browned and crispy.

Serve immediately.

Baby Carrot Tzimmes

Tzimmes is a very traditional Jewish food …
but your Bubby probably made hers from ordinary carrots …

Let's get to it!

3 cups frozen baby carrots
4 prunes
¼ cup raisins, any color
¼ cup sugar
2 tablespoons honey
2 cups water
2 teaspoons potato starch

 Pareve

 Serves 4

And here's how you do it!

1 Put the baby carrots into a pot. Add the water, sugar and honey. Cover the pot.

2 Turn on the fire, and cook for an hour and a half until soft. Check it once in a while to make sure the water does not boil out. You do not want the carrots to burn. If the water does boil out, add more water.

3 Cut up the prunes into four pieces each. Add them to the pot, together with the raisins. Cook for another few minutes.

4 Put the potato starch into a little bowl. Add 2 tablespoons of water, and mix it with a spoon so it won't be lumpy.

5 Add this to the cooking tzimmes. Stir. It should now become thick.

6 Turn off the fire and enjoy your tzimmes.

Latkes & Kugels

Zucchini Kugel

Let's get to it!

3 big zucchini
1 potato
3 eggs
2 tablespoons onion soup mix
2 tablespoons mayonnaise
2 tablespoons potato starch or matzah meal

Pareve

Serves 3–4

And here's how you do it!

1 Preheat the oven to 350°F (180°C).

2 Peel the zucchini and potato and cut into large chunks.

3 Add the zucchini and potatoes to a large pot and cover with water. Turn on the fire and boil for 40 minutes until they are soft. Drain and mash the vegetables, then drain slightly again.

4 Add the rest of the ingredients and mix well.

5 Pour the mixture into a lined 8x8-inch pan and bake until firm in the center, about 45 minutes. The top of the kugel should be browned when it is done. Serve hot.

This slices best cold; to do this, cover the kugel after it has cooled down, refrigerate until it is cold, and then slice. Re-warm for 10 minutes before serving.

Potato Latkes

You can make these with or without the matzah meal; each way comes out great and just a bit different from the other.

Let's get to it!

4 potatoes
1 onion
3 eggs
¼ cup matzah meal
1 teaspoon salt
⅛ teaspoon pepper
Oil for frying

 Pareve

 Serves 3–4

And here's how you do it!

6   Using your food processor fitted with the "S" blade, puree the onion together with the eggs. Pour this into a bowl.

7   Change the blade to the shredder. Grate the potatoes with the shredding blade. Squeeze the grated potatoes with your hands to take out some of the juice. Add the squeezed potatoes to your egg/onion mix.

8   Add the matzah meal, salt, and pepper. Mix together.

9   Heat a frying pan with some of the oil. Put spoonfuls of the potato batter into the frying pan and let them sizzle. When they get brown on the first side, flip them over with a spatula and press them down so they will sizzle on the second side. They are done when they're crispy on both sides.

10 Remove the latkes to a plate covered with paper towels (to absorb some of the oil). Continue making latkes until all your batter is finished.

Save this recipe to use again on Chanukah!

Cheese Latkes

I make these the rest of the year also; whenever I do, everyone asks for seconds.
I never have any left over!

Let's get to it!

1 cup sour cream or 1 container
  (250 grams) 5% Israeli white cheese
1 cup cottage cheese
½ cup sugar
2 eggs
1 cup matzah meal
2 teaspoons baking powder
2 teaspoons vanilla extract
1 teaspoon cinnamon, optional

 Dairy

 Serves 4

And here's how you do it!

1 Mix all ingredients in a bowl by hand, or, for a really smooth texture, blend them with a hand mixer.

2 Matzah meal can be a bit different from one company to the next; therefore, if your pancake batter is very stiff, add a bit of milk to the batter. If it is too runny, add another tablespoon of matzah meal.

3 Spray a frying pan with cooking oil spray and turn on the flame. Spoon the cheese mixture by small ladlefuls into the frying pan.

4 When the pancake is browned on the bottom (it should take about 4 minutes), flip it over to brown on the second side.

5 Remove the cheese pancakes to a serving dish.

Serve immediately. Tastes great as is or with strawberry or blueberry preserves.

Potato Kugel

EVERYBODY, and I do mean everybody, has just got to know how to make a potato kugel. It's one of the most traditional Passover, and also Jewish, kugels on the planet!

Let's get to it!

6 potatoes
1 large onion
4 eggs
1 teaspoon salt
¼ teaspoon pepper
¼ cup oil

 Pareve

 Serves 4

And here's how you do it!

1 Pour ¼ cup oil into an 8x11-inch baking pan so the whole bottom of the pan has oil on it.

2 Preheat the oven to 375°F (190°C).

3 Fit the food processor with the "S" blade and puree the onion together with the eggs. Pour it into a bowl.

4 Change the blade to the shredder. Grate the potatoes with the shredding blade. Squeeze the grated potatoes with your hands to take out some of the juice. Add the squeezed potatoes to the egg/onion mix.

5 Add the salt and pepper. Mix together with a fork.

6 Line the oven rack with a piece of foil to catch any oil that spills over. Pour the mixture into the oiled pan. Slide the pan into the hot oven, on top of the piece of foil, and let it bake for 45–60 minutes, until the top is browned and crispy.

7 When it is sufficiently crunchy on top, take it out, cut pieces for everyone, and bite in! Delicious!

Butternut Squash Kugel

Let's get to it!

2½ cups butternut squash,
  cooked and mashed
⅝ cup potato starch
½ cup oil
½ cup sugar
3 eggs
2 teaspoons cinnamon

 Pareve

GF *Gluten-free!*

 Serves 8

And here's how you do it!

1 Cut 2 medium butternut squashes in half the long way; place them in a large pot with about 4 inches of water, and cover the pot.

2 Turn on the flame and boil the squashes for 40 minutes until are soft. Cool.

3 Scoop the squash out of the peel, and throw out the peel. Mash the squash and measure the amount needed. (Tip: Any extra squash can easily be frozen and used later in a vegetable soup.)

4 Preheat the oven to 350°F (180°C).

5 Sift the potato starch over the mashed squash with a small sifter or tea strainer. (This prevents lumps.) Add the oil, sugar, and eggs. Mix well.

6 Pour the batter into an 8x11-inch baking pan. Sprinkle the cinnamon over the top of the kugel.

7 Bake for 40–45 minutes until the center of the kugel tests firm (it will still be a little wet; that is fine) when pierced with a knife.

This kugel slices neatest when it is cold. Make it one day in advance. The next day, slice it into neat squares and then it can be served cold or warmed up again, covered, for 10 minutes before serving.

Fruity Desserts

Apple Compote

Many, many people serve this old-fashioned, traditional cooked fruit as a dessert for their Passover Seders (before the Afikomen, of course!) ...

Let's get to it!

10 apples
2 teaspoons lemon juice
1 cinnamon stick
½ cup sugar
2 cups water, or 1 cup water +
1 cup semi-dry white wine

 Pareve

 Serves 4

And here's how you do it!

1 Peel and slice all the apples. Put them in a large pot.

2 Add the lemon juice, cinnamon stick, sugar and water. Ask an adult to turn the fire on high so the apples will start to boil.

3 After it boils, turn down the fire to low, cover the pot and let it cook for 45 minutes to one hour. Your home should smell amazing by now.

4 Turn off the fire and put your compote into a plastic container.

5 Refrigerate until it is completely cold. Serve in small dishes.

This compote is also traditionally served for dessert on Friday nights but can be eaten at any time. It's even nicer served together with a scoop of vanilla ice cream — see the recipe on page 84!

Homemade Applesauce

Let's get to it!

10 red, sweet apples
¼ teaspoon salt
½ cup sugar, optional
I stick cinnamon
I cup water

 Pareve

 Serves 4

And here's how we do it!

1 Peel and slice all the apples. Put them in a big pot together with everything else.

2 The sugar is optional, since if the apples are sweet, it is healthier to make this without sugar.

3 Turn the flame on high until it boils, then turn it down, cover the pot and let it cook for 45 minutes. Turn off the flame.

4 Remove the cinnamon stick with a slotted spoon.

5 Using a hand blender, blend the applesauce. If you like it chunky, blend it only partway. If you like it smooth, blend it completely.

6 Refrigerate until you are ready to serve it.

This freezes well.

If you like flavored (and colored!) applesauce, you can always choose one of these flavors:

*For **PURPLE** applesauce, add I cup frozen or fresh blueberries to your applesauce right before you blend it.*

*For **LIGHT ORANGE** applesauce, add 4 canned peach halves or 4 very ripe peaches to your applesauce right before you blend it.*

*For **PINKISH-RED** applesauce, add I–2 cups of strawberries to your applesauce right before you blend it.*

I'm just going to pieces over this yummy recipe!

Crunchy Cranberry Relish

Let's get to it!

- 1 package red jello
- 1 cup boiling water
- 1 cup applesauce
- 1 can cranberry sauce
- ½ cup chopped walnuts
- 1 cup crushed pineapple
- 1 small can mandarin oranges without the juice

 Pareve

 Serves 6

And here's how you do it!

1 Open the jello package and pour the powder into a bowl. Add the boiling water and stir so it won't be lumpy. Put it in the fridge to set for 15 minutes.

2 After the 15 minutes, add the applesauce and the cranberry sauce. (You can use cranberry sauce with or without the berries in it, depending on what you prefer.) Using a fork, mash the mixture together in a bowl.

3 Add the walnuts, pineapple and mandarin orange pieces. Mix everything together.

4 Put the relish into a plastic container and refrigerate.
This is a great side dish to a meaty meal; it goes especially well alongside turkey or meat.

This freezes well.

Blended Fruit Soup

Let's get to it!

8 overripe plums, pitted
6 canned peach halves
   or 4-5 fresh ripened peaches, pitted
5 apricots, pitted
I cup grapes, optional
3 apples, peeled and sliced
I cup blueberries, fresh or frozen
3 cups water
¾ cup sugar
I teaspoon lemon juice
I cup orange juice, saved for later

 Pareve

 Serves 6

And here's how you do it!

1 Take out a large pot. Cut up all the fruits — the plums, peaches, apricots and apples — and add them into the pot. Throw away all the pits and seeds from the fruit.

2 Add the blueberries and grapes.

3 Add the water, sugar and lemon juice.

4 Put the pot on a high flame. Cover the pot and let it boil. Once the soup is bubbling, turn it down to simmer and let it cook for 45 minutes to an hour. The soup should smell amazing while it's cooking!

5 When the fruit soup is done, turn off the fire. Add the orange juice.

6 Cool the soup for half an hour. Blend with an immersion blender until it is smooth and thick.

7 Chill in the fridge overnight.

Serve in soup bowls or tall glasses and watch everyone enjoy it down to the last drop!

Stuffed Baked Apples

Let's get to it!

4 large apples
4 prunes
¼ cup raisins
1 cup orange juice
1 teaspoon cinnamon
2 teaspoons sugar

 Pareve

 Serves 4

And here's how you do it!

1   Take out a glass baking dish. Preheat the oven to 375°F (190°C).

2   Wash off the apples and core them with an apple corer. This way each apple stays whole but has a neat hole down its center.

3   Stuff one prune into each apple's "hole" to close up the bottom of it. Stuff some raisins into each apple, on top of the prune.

4   Pour some orange juice over all the apples and make sure to drip some into each apple's hole as well.

5   Mix the cinnamon and sugar in a little bowl with a spoon. Sprinkle the cinnamon/sugar mixture on top of each apple.

6   Cover the baking dish tightly with parchment paper and then foil. Slide the dish into the hot oven and bake until the apples are softened, about one hour.

Serve hot (with vanilla ice cream, if you like!) or refrigerate them and serve them cold a few hours later. Either way, these are super-yum!

Catch that runaway cake!

Fruit Cups

Let's get to it!

| ¼ of a watermelon |
| ⅓ of a cantaloupe |
| ⅓ of a small honeydew |
| I small fresh pineapple |
| or I small can pineapple chunks |
| I cup fresh blueberries |
| ¼ cup shredded coconut |
| 8 cherries |

 Pareve

 Serves 4

And here's how you do it!

1 Use a fruit baller for the best results. It's fun and easy to use, and you'll love the way it looks when you're done!

2 Take out four pretty and somewhat larger glass dessert cups or glasses on stems for this recipe.

3 Take out an ordinary large bowl.

4 Using the fruit baller, make balls out of the watermelon, cantaloupe and honeydew. Put them all into the large bowl.

5 Cut the pineapple into small chunks and add to the bowl. Add the blueberries. Toss together with a large spoon.

6 Scoop the fruit into the prepared glasses. Sprinkle with some of the shredded coconut. Top each glass with 2 cherries and serve.

Frozen Raisin Clusters

Let's get to it!

1 cup yellow raisins
1 cup dark raisins
8 oz. (250 grams) non-dairy (pareve),
   semi-sweetened chocolate
Little paper cupcake holders

 Pareve

 Serves 6

And here's how you do it!

1 Put the chocolate in a small saucepan. Melt it over very low heat.

2 Keep stirring it with a wooden spoon so it doesn't burn. When it is mostly melted, but not completely, turn off the fire. Continue stirring it off the fire; now it will melt on its own.

3 Add the raisins. Stir together.

4 Prepare about 15 paper cupcake holders on a flat baking pan.

5 Using a spoon, spoon some of the chocolate-raisin mix into each little cup.

6 Continue doing this until all the little cups are filled halfway. You may have more portions than listed.

7 Slide the pan into the freezer, and freeze for a few hours.

Serve frozen.

Coated Banana Freeze Pops

Let's get to it!

4 ripe bananas (but not too overripe)
4–5 oz. / 100 gram bar non-dairy
   semi-sweet chocolate
½ cup very finely ground nuts
   (almonds, walnuts or candied pecans)
½ cup chocolate sprinkles
Wooden skewers, one per banana

 Pareve

 Serves 8

And here's how you do it!

1. The day before you want to do this, peel four ripe bananas. Cut each one in half and put a skewer into the fatter end of each one and lay them flat on a paper-lined cookie sheet. Freeze them overnight.

2. Now prepare your "dips."

3. Put the finely ground nuts into one little bowl.

4. Put the sprinkles into another little bowl.

5. Melt the chocolate in a small pot, until it is liquidy. Be careful not to heat it too high or it will burn.

6. Place the bananas on a piece of parchment paper on your table. Dip each banana top into the melted chocolate. Now dip the chocolate end into your dip of choice, either the nuts or the sprinkles. Lay them down on the paper to harden.

7. Refreeze the banana pops again for another half hour so they will harden once more.

Give each friend or sister or brother one banana pop, start lickin' and enjoy!

Poached Pears

Let's get to it!

8–10 medium pears
½ cup semi-dry red wine
½ cup sugar
1 package red jello
1 cinnamon stick or ½ teaspoon cinnamon
Water

 Pareve

 Serves 6–8

And here's how you do it!

1 Peel the pears and rinse them off, but leave the stems on if you can.

2 Put them all into a pot, in one layer.

3 Add the wine, sugar, jello and cinnamon stick.

4 Cover the pears with water and cover the pot.

5 Turn on the fire and bring the pears to a boil.

6 Cook the pears over a small fire so it bubbles gently, for 45 minutes. They should be soft but not mushy.

7 Put the poached pears in a plastic container and refrigerate them until they are cold.

Your pears will be a great hit! They are tasty, and will be two-colored when they are sliced open, soft pink on the outside, white on the inside …

These pears also freeze well.

Strawberry Soup

Let's get to it!

1 16 oz. package frozen strawberries
2 cups pineapple tidbits,
    with ¼ cup of the juice
¼ cup sugar, or to taste
1 cup orange juice
½ cup seltzer

  Pareve

Serves 6

And here's how you do it!

1 Defrost the strawberries for 10 minutes so they soften a bit.

2 Place the strawberries and pineapple tidbits into the food processor.

3 Add the pineapple juice, sugar, orange juice and seltzer and blend together until smooth and thick.

4 Pour into tall glasses until 1 inch below the top of the glass.

5 Place one ice cube and a straw into each glass.

Serve and watch your guests ooh in delight!

And here's a great serving tip: Serve this drink with a round slice of fresh orange hung on the edge of each glass.

Cakes, Cookies, and Mmm ... More!

Many people think that Passover is a time when there is "nothing to serve for dessert" or that the cakes "all come out dry and tasteless." Well, with these great recipes, I hope to get rid of these silly complaints once and for all ...

Blondies

I got this recipe from my sister's friend, Tova Wechsler

Let's get to it!

4 eggs
1½ cups sugar
1 cup oil
3 teaspoons vanilla extract
1 cup potato starch
3 teaspoons baking powder
⅔ cup ground almonds
1 cup chocolate chips

 Pareve

 Serves 10–12

And here's how you do it!

1 Preheat the oven to 350°F (180°C).

2 Mix the eggs, sugar, and oil.

3 Add the vanilla extract, potato starch, baking powder and ground nuts.

4 Pour this batter into a lined 9x13-inch baking pan.

5 Sprinkle the top with chocolate chips. Push them down part way into the batter.

6 Bake for 45 minutes until it is done in the center.

7 Cut into squares when cool.

You can also sprinkle it with powdered sugar before serving for a nice effect.

Rocky Road Brownies

"INCREDIBLE" doesn't even come close to describing this! And it freezes well, too!

Let's get to it!

4 oz. (115 grams) semi-sweet
chocolate, chopped
1 cup (200 grams or 2 American sticks)
margarine or 1 cup oil
1½ cups sugar
4 eggs
1 cup matzah cake meal
½ teaspoon salt
1 cup chocolate chips
2 cups mini marshmallows
1 cup walnuts, chopped

Topping:
1 cup mini marshmallows
½ cup chocolate chips
½ cup walnuts, coarsely ground

 Pareve

 Serves 10

And here's how you do it!

1 Preheat the oven to 325°F (160°C). Prepare a 9x13-inch pan by lining it
with parchment paper or spraying it well with cooking oil spray.

2 Melt the chopped chocolate and margarine in a double boiler and stir
well. Stir in the sugar. Cool slightly.

3 Whisk in the eggs one at a time. Stir in the cake meal and salt,
and remove the pot from the heat. Stir in the chocolate chips,
marshmallows and walnuts.

4 Pour this batter into the prepared baking pan and bake for 30 minutes
or until set. Remove the pan from the oven, and sprinkle the brownies
with the additional cup of marshmallows.

5 Slide the tray back into the oven and bake 3–4 minutes more, until the
marshmallows are puffed. Remove the pan from the oven and melt the
second set of chocolate chips.

6 Drizzle the melted chips all over the brownies and then sprinkle them,
while the chocolate is still wet, with the last bit of ground nuts.

Cut into squares and serve.

Chocolate Chip Brownies

Let's get to it!

6 eggs
2⅔ cups sugar
1½ cups potato starch
¾ cup cocoa
¾ cup oil
1 teaspoon vanilla extract
1 cup white or dark chocolate chips

Chocolate Glaze:
1 cup powdered sugar
2 tablespoons oil
2 tablespoons cocoa
2 tablespoons hot water

 Pareve

 GF *Gluten-free!*

 Serves 10–12

And here's how you do it!

1 Preheat the oven to 350°F (180°C). Line a 9x13-inch baking pan with parchment paper.

2 Put the eggs, sugar, potato starch, cocoa, oil and vanilla extract into a mixing bowl. Mix them together until they are smooth, using a hand mixer or your arms and a strong spoon! Add the chocolate chips and mix again.

3 Pour the batter into the prepared baking pan. Smooth out the top with a spoon. Slide the pan into the oven and bake for 30–40 minutes. The brownies should be firm but still a bit moist in the center. The edges will get crispy, but don't let it burn.

4 Remove the pan from the oven and let it cool completely.

5 When the brownies are cooled, mix the glaze ingredients together in a small bowl. Mix it with a spoon until it is smooth and thick enough to spread. (It should be as thick as peanut butter.) Pour the glaze over the brownies and smear it all over with the back of a large spoon. DON'T do this while the brownies are still hot or even warm; it will sink into the brownies that way!

6 Freeze the brownies. When they are semi-frozen, cut into squares and serve.

Passover Apple Crisp

Never knew you could do a great apple crisp without margarine and even better, without flour? And if you want to, even without gluten? (See the * below.) Well, now you know it's possible! We do this one every Pesach; it is so outstanding ...

Let's get to it!

Filling:
5 tart apples, peeled and sliced
2 tablespoons lemon juice
¼ cup sugar
½ teaspoon cinnamon

 Pareve

 Serves 6

Crumbs:
½ cup sugar
1 cup matzah meal*
1 teaspoon cinnamon
½ cup oil
½ cup chopped almonds
½ cup chopped walnuts

And here's how you do it!

1 Lightly oil a 9x11-inch glass baking dish. Preheat the oven to 350°F (180°C).

2 Peel all the apples and slice thinly. Place the sliced apples in a bowl.

3 Add the lemon juice, sugar, and cinnamon. Toss them together so all the apples are coated.

4 In a different bowl, combine the ingredients for the crumb topping. Mix with a fork until the crumbs look like ... crumbs!

5 Put the apple mixture into the baking dish. Sprinkle the crumb mix evenly over the apples in the pan.

6 Slide the baking dish into the oven and bake for 40–45 minutes or until pan juices start to bubble up through the topping. The topping should be crispy and lightly browned.

7 Let it cool, then cover with foil and refrigerate until you are ready to serve it.

* *If you want to make this gluten-free, use 1 cup potato starch instead of the matzah meal. It really works well!*

Passover Mock Oatmeal Cookies

Let's get to it!

3 eggs
¾ cup oil
1 cup matzah meal
1 cup matzah farfel
1 cup sugar
½ teaspoon cinnamon
1 teaspoon baking soda
½ cup raisins + 1 teaspoon additional matzah meal
⅓ cup chocolate chips
½ cup chopped walnuts (not finely ground)

 Pareve

 Makes about 24 cookies

And here's how you do it!

1 Preheat the oven to 350°F (180°C).

2 Beat the eggs in a mixer. Add the oil and continue beating.

3 Add the matzah meal, matzah farfel, sugar, cinnamon and baking soda to the eggs. It should be a thick mixture.

4 Sprinkle 1 teaspoon matzah meal on the raisins and then fold the raisins, chocolate chips and nuts into the mixture by hand.

5 Line cookie sheets with parchment paper.

6 Drop the cookie mixture by teaspoonfuls onto the cookie sheet, or roll them into balls and flatten them slightly after you place them on the cookie sheet.

7 Bake the cookies for 15 minutes or until they are slightly browned on top and bottom.

They freeze well, of course, if you can manage to get any in the freezer before everyone comes by and starts to eat them all up …

Baked today, gone tomorrow …

Chocolate Chip Cookies

And who doesn't just LOVE a good chocolate chip cookie? This makes about 45 cookies – or so. Hard to tell as they get eaten very quickly!

Let's get to it!

2 cups sugar
2 eggs
1 cup oil
2 tablespoons vanilla sugar
3¼ cups (400 grams) almond flour
1 cup potato starch
1¼ cups (300 grams) chocolate chips

 Pareve

 GF *Gluten-free!*

 Makes about 45 cookies

And here's how you do it!

1   Preheat the oven to 350°F (180°C). Line a cookie sheet with parchment paper.

2   Cream together the sugar, eggs, and oil. Add the vanilla sugar, almond flour, and potato starch and mix well. Add the chocolate chips and stir with a spoon.

3   Freeze the batter for 10–20 minutes to make it easier to form the cookies. It will be oily, but this is normal.

4   Make small balls out of the batter using your hands or a mini ice-cream scooper. Place the balls on the cookie sheet.

5   DO NOT flatten the cookies at all. They spread a lot in the baking process.

6   Bake them for 12 minutes, until they are lightly browned and crinkled.

7   Let them cool a bit on the paper before removing.

Hide them quickly if you want some for later, and yes, these do freeze well!

Desserts, Shakes & Drinks

Strawberry Snow

Let's get to it!

- ½ lb. (250 grams) frozen strawberries
- ½ cup sugar
- ⅛ teaspoon lemon juice
- 2 egg whites

Pareve

Serves 6

And here's how you do it!

1. Put the strawberries, sugar and lemon juice into a food processor. Puree everything until smooth.

2. Place the egg whites into the mixer bowl. Beat on high until they turn white and begin to stiffen.

3. Turn down the mixer's speed a bit and while it is still beating, slowly pour in the pureed strawberry mixture.

4. You should see the egg whites begin to turn pink and grow higher!

5. Once all the strawberries are mixed in, turn off the mixer.

6. Pour it into a container and freeze for several hours or overnight.

Scoop out portions and enjoy!

Chocolate Mousse

My kids make this for us every year … mmmm …

Let's get to it!

8 eggs, separated
8 oz. (225 grams) semisweet chocolate
1 tablespoon instant coffee
   with ¼ cup hot water
⅔ cup sugar
1 teaspoon vanilla extract

 Pareve

 Serves 6–8

And here's how you do it!

1 Separate the eggs; put the whites into a mixing bowl. Using a mixer, beat the egg whites until they are white and fluffy. Slowly add half the sugar. When the whites are stiff and high, turn off the mixer.

2 Melt the chocolate on a very low flame; stir it while it is melting so it will not burn.

3 Put the coffee into the hot water and stir to dissolve. Add this to the melted chocolate and mix together until there are no lumps.

4 Place the egg yolks into another mixer bowl. Beat on high speed, together with the rest of the sugar, until it becomes light yellow and thick.

5 Add the melted chocolate/coffee to the yolks. Beat a bit more until it is well combined. Turn off the mixer.

6 Use a large rubber spatula to fold the whites into the yolk/chocolate mixture. This is the mousse! It will be liquidy — that's okay. Pour into a container and refrigerate it overnight so it will thicken.

For a nice serving idea, divide the mousse into individual tall glasses or dessert dishes. Once the mousse is firm you can top each one with any or all of these ideas:

A scoop of vanilla ice cream, page 84

A dollop of whipped cream plus a few blueberries

Some crumbled brownie crumbs can go on the bottom of each glass, then put the mousse on top and then the whipped cream

Or freeze the mousse and serve it like a rich chocolate ice cream

Marshmallow Dream Ice Cream

Let's get to it!

8 eggs, separated
1 cup sugar
⅔ cup oil
4 teaspoons vanilla sugar
1½ cups mini marshmallows
Chocolate or colored sprinkles, optional

 Pareve

 Serves 8

And here's how you do it!

1 Separate the eggs. Put the whites into a large mixing bowl. Beat on high speed until they begin to turn white and stiff. Turn down the mixer speed and add the sugar, oil, yolks and vanilla sugar.

2 Pour half of the ice cream batter into a large plastic container. Sprinkle half of the mini-marshmallows on top.

3 Pour the rest of the ice cream batter into the container and layer the top with the rest of the marshmallows. You can also add the sprinkles to the top of the ice cream now.

4 Freeze overnight. Serve in scoops in pretty glass bowls.

Always be sure to close the fridge door ...

Easy Vanilla Ice Cream

Let's get to it!

8–9 eggs, separated
1 cup sugar
½ cup oil (*not* olive oil)
3 teaspoons vanilla sugar

 Pareve

 Serves 6–8

And here's how you do it!

1. Separate the eggs. Put the whites into a large mixing bowl. Beat on high speed until they begin to turn white and stiff.

2. Add the yolks into the beating whites, then the sugar, oil and vanilla sugar. As soon as it is all mixed together, turn off the mixer.

3. Pour the ice cream batter into a large plastic (not metal) container and freeze.

*For **Vanilla Chocolate Swirl** ice cream, simply pour half of the batter into the pan or container. Drizzle chocolate syrup all over it and then layer the rest of the batter on top, adding more chocolate syrup on the top. Freeze. When you scoop it out, the chocolate swirls will be quite evident!*

Chocolate Chip Ice Cream

Wow your family and friends with this great ice cream, and you can even have it for dessert after eating a meat meal — looks so real you'll never believe it's not dairy!

Let's get to it!

10 eggs, separated
1 cup sugar
½ cup oil
3 teaspoons vanilla sugar
1 cup mini chocolate chips
Chocolate syrup, optional

 Pareve

 Serves 8

And here's how you do it!

1 Separate the eggs.

2 Put the whites into a large mixing bowl. Beat on high speed until they begin to turn white and stiff.

3 Add the yolks into the beating whites. Add the sugar, oil and vanilla sugar. As soon as it is all mixed together, turn off the mixer.

4 Pour half of the ice cream batter into a large plastic (not metal) container.

5 Drizzle on some of the chocolate syrup, if desired. Sprinkle on half of the chocolate chips.

6 Pour the rest of the ice cream batter into the pan and layer the top with more syrup and the rest of the chips.

7 Freeze overnight.

Chocolate-Coffee Ice Cream

Let's get to it!

6 eggs, separated
1 cup sugar
½ cup oil
2 teaspoons cocoa
2 teaspoon coffee
1 teaspoon vanilla extract
4 tablespoons crushed chocolate chips

 Pareve

 Serves 6–8

And here's how you do it!

1 Separate the eggs. Beat the whites until they begin to turn white; slowly add the sugar while you continue beating.

2 In another bowl, beat the yolks until they turn light and thick. Add the oil, cocoa, coffee and vanilla extract and beat a bit more.

3 Fold whites into yolk mixture with a large spatula. Add the chocolate chips and fold them in. Freeze until solid, and then scoop and serve.

Ice Cream Sundae

Let's get to it!

3 ripe (but not brown) bananas
3 scoops vanilla ice cream
3 scoops chocolate ice cream
3 teaspoons chocolate sprinkles
3 teaspoons shredded coconut
3 teaspoons ground nuts
Chocolate syrup
Whipped cream

 Pareve

 Serves 3

And here's how you do it!

1 Take out three bowls. Slice each banana in half the long way. Put two halves into each bowl. Put one scoop of vanilla and one of chocolate ice cream into the middle of the banana halves in each bowl.

2 Sprinkle on the sprinkles, coconut and ground nuts. Drizzle some syrup over each one. Squirt on some whipped cream and enjoy!

Incredible Milkshakes

Let's get to it!

2 cups milk
2 frozen bananas (*When you have some ripened bananas, peel them and put them into plastic bags. Freeze them. Now, whenever you want a milkshake, all you have to do is take the bananas out of the freezer …*)

 Dairy

 Serves 2

And here's how you do it!

1 Put the milk in the blender.

2 Break the bananas up into smaller chunks and add into the blender. Let it sit for 5 minutes to soften somewhat.

3 Cover the blender and blend on high until the shake is creamy and smooth.

4 Serve in tall glasses with straws and drink away …

Add 5–6 frozen strawberries to your milkshake and watch it turn pink!

*Add ½ cup frozen blueberries to your milkshake and watch it turn **purple**!*

Add ½ of a very ripe mango to your shake and it will turn light orange … and be very yummy, besides!

Leftovers? You gotta be kidding!

Milk-Less Fruit Shakes

A great and healthy shake that comes out creamy and thick — without the milk! Good for a refresher after a meaty meal, or for those who are lactose-intolerant …

Let's get to it!

- 2 frozen bananas
- 3 cups orange juice
- ½ cup blueberries
- 8 frozen strawberries

 Pareve

 Serves 4

And here's how you do it!

1 Chop the bananas into small pieces and put them into the blender.

2 Pour the orange juice over the bananas. Add the blueberries and strawberries. Let it sit together for five to ten minutes, so it softens somewhat.

3 Cover the blender and blend on high until it is smooth and thick.

4 Pour into four tall glasses.

Add straws, and for a pretty presentation, you can sprinkle a few whole blueberries into the center of each glass. Also, you can substitute one cup of the orange juice with seltzer and it will be a bit fizzy.

Cleaning up when you're done is part of the fun!

Homemade Ice Coffee

Let's get to it!

1–2 cups 3% milk
3 cups pre-frozen milk*
2 tablespoons instant decaf coffee
¼ cup dark brown (or white) sugar
2 tablespoons instant vanilla pudding powder
Straws
Tall glasses

 Dairy

 Serves 3–4

* The night before you want to make this (in a pinch it even works if done several hours before), take four plastic disposable cups and fill each with ¾ cup milk. Freeze until solid.

And here's how you do it!

1 Place 1–2 cups milk into the blender.

2 Add the frozen milk, removed from the plastic cups. To release the milk from the cups easily either take them out of the freezer half an hour before using, or run the cups under a stream of water and then the frozen milk will just pop out.

3 Add the instant coffee, sugar and vanilla powder.

4 Let it sit in the blender for about 10 minutes, so that the frozen milk will defrost a bit and soften up somewhat.

5 If it's too hard and frozen, it could break your blender, so beware!

6 To test that the frozen milk is ready to be blended, just cut each in half with a knife. If they cut easily, they're ready.

7 Now, turn on your blender, pause, and blend again.

Pour your ice coffee into glasses, insert your straws and … enjoy!

Fresh Lemonade

Let's get to it!

2 large lemons
1 cup sugar
2 quarts water
Ice cubes

 Pareve

 Serves 4

And here's how you do it!

1 Squeeze the lemons. Save some of the pulp. Throw out the rinds and the seeds. Pour the lemon juice into a large pitcher.

2 Add the water. Add the sugar and stir together.

3 Put the pitcher into the fridge for an hour or so. Stir again before serving. Add some ice cubes and enjoy!

To make it fancier, scrub off the outside of another lemon. Slice it into rounds and add one or two rounds to the outside of the pitcher, hanging off the side.

Fro-Yo Ice Pops

Let's get to it!

3 plain yogurts
8 frozen strawberries
½ cup blueberries
2 tablespoons honey

 Dairy

 Serves 4

And here's how you do it!

1 Blend the yogurts with the strawberries, blueberries and honey.

2 Pour into a popsicle mold that has four to six slots in it. If you don't have a popsicle mold, pour it into a few plastic cups, filling each cup halfway. Put a popsicle stick or a plastic spoon into each cup for your handle. Freeze until solid.

3 Take it out, start licking and enjoy!

Fun Arts & Crafts

Here are some fun things you can make yourself. You'll be proud to bring them to your Seder table and present them to the relatives you made them for!

Passover Aprons

This is something you can either make just for yourself to wear, since you will now be a great cook, or ... how about making two aprons? Then your grandmother, mother or friend can be matching with you when you're in the kitchen together!

Let's get to it!

I or 2 plain white cloth aprons
Package permanent magic markers
Colorful puff paints
Any iron-on design you pick out from a crafts store

And here's how you do it!

1 Try on the apron, and note with a pencil where the apron lays on you closest to your center, right between the rib cages.

2 Think of a title for yourself and put that in the center of the apron. Be creative and do something fun like "The Greatest Passover Cook!" "Cook Hard at Work – Beware!" "Master Chef in Charge – Look Out!" or anything creative you can think up. If you're making your mom or gradma a matching one, you can write on it, "Master Cook's Helper" or anything else that is a private joke between you and her.

3 Place the apron on a flat, clean surface. Decide where you want the iron-on decal — in the middle, the pocket or near the bottom — and leave space for it. Using your magic markers, draw some matzahs, butterflies, flowers, Kiddush cups or any other Passover symbols all over the apron.

4　Use your puffy paints to decorate your apron further. It's a good idea, whenever you color fabric with puffy paints or magic markers, to put some paper underneath the area you are working on. This way, when the paint or markers go through the fabric, it will not go through to the second side.

5　Take your time so it will come out nice, and enjoy wearing — and using — it! At the end of Passover you can wash the apron and put it away with the Passover things, so you can use it again next year.

Passover Placemats

I came up with this idea years ago when I was a pre-kindergarten teacher, and I also made them with my own kids when they were small. When they were finished, we gave them to their grandparents and it was such a hit! It was a great present for a grandparent, because aside from being useful, all grandparents wants to look at pictures of their grandkids all the time, and this fit both requirements quite nicely ...

Let's get to it!

One sturdy, brightly colored piece of thicker construction paper, size 8X11 (A4), per kid
One good photo of each kid who is making a placemat
Stickers for decorating the edges
Magic markers in various colors
Stencil for writing the letters of the name, optional

And here's how you do it!

1　Using the stencil, if you have it, write your name neatly near the top right half of the paper. You can do it in Hebrew or English letters.

2　Attach the photo to the other half of the paper.

3　Place stickers in any pattern you like all around the edges of the paper; this will be your border or frame.

4　Using the magic markers, color the name and the rest of the paper so it will be pretty. Those who know how to write can add a short love note to the person who will be receiving the placemat, such as, "Hi, Bubby, I love you! Happy Pesach!"

5　When you are done, take it to a store that does lamination and laminate it. Now your placemat is all ready for use! When it gets dirty, just give it a swipe with a damp rag, and it will be as good as new!

Seder Table Pillows

This one requires a bit of planning, but it is very cute when you are all done. You can do this on your own, or with any age siblings or friends, even those as young as three years old.

Let's get to it!

White cloth that, when folded in half, should become an 8- or 9-inch square; or a plain white, or solid color, cotton-blend pillowcase
Thread
Puff paints
Permanent magic markers
Hebrew letter stencils for medium sized letters

And here's how you do it!

1 Get a parent or a friend who knows how to sew to help you out. All she has to do is cut the cloth so that when it is done, it will be a square of about 8–9 inches large and will be closed on three sides, leaving the fourth side open.

2 Get tons of scraps of cloth from a material store that wants to get rid of extras, or from anyone you know who enjoys sewing. If you can't get this, ask your mother for two very old sheets. This will be your stuffing.

3 Put a piece of paper or something inside the cloth before you do the lettering, so that the marker does not come through to the other side. Using a black permanent magic marker and a stencil, or just your own handwriting, write in Hebrew letters: לכבוד ליל הסדר ("Lichvod Leil HaSeder," which means, "In honor of the Seder night") across the middle of the front of the pillowcase.

4 Decorate the letters, color them in, etc. with your permanent markers. If it's young children doing this, they will scribble but that's okay — this is how they enjoy coloring at their age. Don't do it for them; let them scribble and have a good time. Leave the paper inside the pillow while you/they are doing this so the coloring will not be all over the back.

5 When you are done, stuff the pillow as much as possible with the cloth scraps (best) or with the one or two old sheets your mom gave you. If she lets you, you can cut up the sheets to make it more manageable. Ask first! Cloth is best as it is both soft and washable.

6 Sew up the open end of the pillow.

7 Use the puffy paints to create the rest of your design and, presto, you'll have a unique personalized pillow to lean on at your place for the Passover Sedarim! Best part — it's washable. Just throw it into the washing machine on gentle, wash, and let it air-dry.

Another idea: If the cloth part is too complicated for you, you can easily use this idea with an ordinary, solid-colored pillowcase that you have permission to draw on and decorate. Or ask your mom to take you shopping a few weeks before Passover to get white or solid-colored cotton-blend pillowcases that you can decorate. Then all you need to do to "stuff" it is to slide a real pillow inside it when it's ready for use!

Wine Bottle Labels

How about this for a stunning decoration? We drink four cups of grape juice or wine during each of the Passover Seders. Wouldn't it look special if you made labels for the bottles of wine that will be on your table?

1 On the next page you have four different and beautiful labels. All you have to do is cut this page out of the book, or photocopy it from here.

2 Sit down and cut out each label carefully and exactly.

3 When you're done, simply attach each label to the wine bottles that will be on your table.

Tip: The labels will stick best if you do it on the bottles when they are room temperature. Bottles that have been in the refrigerator become slightly wet when they are taken out and then you may have trouble getting your labels to stick well.

Just cut and tape!

Just one sample from
The Great Pesach Funbook
by Chani Saposh, a Passover
activity book with over 30 fun
games, puzzles, riddles and more!

95

Other books by Tamar Ansh

Tamar Ansh is a busy mom who loves to write, cook, bake, read, and chat with her kids. Since her kids have recently taken over the kitchen, she decided to share what they do with you. In her spare time she is a bestselling author of cookbooks, children's books and adult books, writes recipes for other moms in food columns, and gives live cooking and challah shows all over. Mrs. Ansh lives in Jerusalem together with her family and their pet rabbit Fluffy.

TamarAnsh.com | aTasteofChallah.com
tamar@atasteofchallah.com

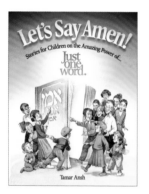

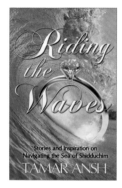